THE MISSING PROFESSOR

THE MISSING PROFESSOR

An Academic Mystery

Thomas B. Jones

STERLING, VIRGINIA

Sty/us

COPYRIGHT © 2006 STYLUS PUBLISHING, LLC

Published by Stylus Publishing, LLC
22883 Quicksilver Drive
Sterling, Virginia 20166-2102

Library of Congress Cataloging-in-Publication Data
Jones, Thomas B., 1942–
    The missing professor : an academic mystery :
informal case studies, discussion stories for faculty
development, new faculty orientation, and campus
conversations / Thomas B. Jones.—1st ed.
        p.   cm.
    ISBN 1-57922-137-8 (hardcover : alk. paper)
    ISBN 1-57922-138-6 (pbk. : alk. paper)
    1. College personnel management.   2. Teacher-
administrator relationships.   I. Title.
LB2331.66.J66   2005
378.1′2—dc22   2005020833

ISBN: 1-57922-137-8 (cloth)
ISBN: 1-57922-138-6 (paper)

Printed in Canada

All first editions printed on acid-free paper
that meets the American National Standards Institute
Z39-48 Standard.

First Edition, 2006

10 9 8 7 6 5 4 3 2 1

I dedicate this book to Susan Keiko Nathan, who makes everything right and worthwhile, and to my children Buirge and Jessica, who are the truly talented and funny ones in the family.

Author's Note and Acknowledgments

Some years ago, I wrote a case study/discussion story intended for the first meeting in a semester's series of workshops on college teaching. Much to my delight, the workshop participants—from a range of academic disciplines—enjoyed reading and discussing what I had written. They asked me to follow through with new episodes for future workshop discussions, and I did. The result? Case studies and discussion stories dealing with a variety of topics, from college teaching to faculty roles to general education, all fitted within the framework of a mystery novel.

Read from the front cover, *The Missing Professor* is a mystery story and, I hope, a humorous take on academic life. The book's main purpose, however, is to provide grist for workshops, teaching circles, "brown bag" discussion sessions, new faculty orientation, dreaded "in-service" or presemester meetings, and one-to-one mentoring.

Turning the book upside down, readers will find several pages containing my suggestions on how the book can be used for faculty development. I have no doubt faculty members will jump right into discussions, identifying issues, posing questions, citing resources, and applying professional expertise and experience with little need for directions. But I do hope that some of the things I have worked into this back section of the book will prove useful.

Some of the humor and story lines in *The Missing Professor* will likely not appeal to every reader. So be it. But please understand that the tie-in to *Cannabis sativa* is merely a plot device, hardly a recommendation for its use.

I wish to acknowledge the expertise and friendship of Donna Blacker at Metropolitan State University. She has spent many years encouraging, guiding, and improving my attempts at being a good teacher, scholar, and writer. I also want to thank John von Knorring, president of Stylus Press, for his encouragement and wise judgment. Professor Ed Nuhfer of Idaho State University read the manuscript with great care and insight. His comprehensive and exacting review proved invaluable to me. To my friends at Metropolitan State University, Rockhurst University, and Maple Woods College, who have read and discussed parts of this book . . . thank you. Thanks, in particular, to Professors Prudy and Rich Hall, Jessica Dumas, James Murray, Debra McCarty, and Dean Mindy McCallum.

HIGHER STATE UNIVERSITY

"Reach Higher" at HSU

Assistant Professor of Philosophy

HIGHER STATE UNIVERSITY
ESTABLISHED 1978 A.D.

Higher State University welcomes applications for a tenure-track position in the Department of Philosophy. Specialization in **Ethics** and ability to teach key areas of the general education curriculum required. The teaching load is four three-hour classes per semester. Candidates for the position must be devoted to quality undergraduate teaching and advising. Scholarly activity and departmental service are expected. PhD required by time of appointment.

Higher State University is a selective admissions, fully accredited, mid-level, public state university with a progressive tradition and a strategic plan for the future. Our founders envisioned a university dedicated to the best educational ideals and committed to expanding opportunities for undergraduate and graduate students. The university plays host to some 3,000 undergraduate and 100 graduate students. Students enjoy the benefits of relatively small classes and the attention of a devoted faculty, academic staff, and administration. The HSU community is proud of our library, high-technology classrooms, recently repainted dormitories, state-of-the-art waste disposal systems, the new 10,000-seat Bill Lee Athletic Complex, and the DeTassell Harvest Festival.

Higher State University is located in Normal City, the crown jewel of the semi-rolling hills of West Central Iowa. Normal City is one of the state's larger urban areas. Higher State University and the community of Normal City work hand in hand to provide an unusual mix of entertainment, recreational, and cultural opportunities.

Archival Note: Unknown author's handwritten annotation of the Higher State University *2003–2004 Catalog*. Document found in the Raskin Collection, July 2005. HSU University Library Archives.

Early University History

Higher State University was founded in 1976 by a unique consortium of educational idealists.

When the university's administration encountered legal difficulties in the early 1980s, the State University System assumed control over the campus and its programs.

However, prominent alumni and community leaders consented to the state system's action only on the condition that the university would remain known as "Higher State."

The university has retained its founding name with enthusiasm, always asking its administration, faculty, and students to "reach higher" in their pursuit of academic excellence.

In the early 1970s, members of the San Francisco-based "Kaliflower Kommune" made a small fortune selling organic vegetables to hip grocery stores in the Bay Area. At the same time, the group turned its scientific-horticultural talents to the production of very high-quality, high-yield marijuana. Pressed by local authorities about their products, the group's members decided to get back to their roots in the Heartland, especially since their leader, James DeTassell, aka "Silk," hailed from Normal. By virtue of a tragic, though fortunate, coincidence, DeTassell's father, "Spin," had lost his life jousting with a corn thresher—reportedly after imbibing a fifth of whiskey at the Hawkeye Bar and Gentlemen's Fantasy Ranch. (Mrs. DeTassell had long since left "the Mr." in favor of a tent show preacher from Lone Jack, Missouri.) The younger DeTassell inherited the farm and soon had it turning out superlative organic carrots, spinach, and soy products for the vegan, green-tea-sipping liberals in neighboring Minnesota. (However, rumors persist that DeTassell and his friends had also revived their cannabis cultivation.) The farm operation and packaging factory emerged as the major industry in Normal, employing some 65 percent of the local labor force. Profits soaring, DeTassell and several Berkeley PhDs within the Kaliflower Kommune decided to found a university in 1978 dedicated to educational innovation and the reform of American higher education.

A mass raid of combined FBI and Iowa Drug Enforcement officers on the agricultural business program revealed faculty and students had devised new textbook models for production and distribution.

Eschewing his usual low public profile, DeTassell told county and state officials he would pack up his profitable, high-employment growing and manufacturing operations and move if "Higher State" turned into "some half-assed directional school . . . a Northwest Central Iowa State." The "Hippie Entrepreneur," as Time Magazine had dubbed DeTassell in the 1970s, also threatened to cut off private contributions to the governor if "the whole thing goes down." DeTassell vowed he would continue an effort to return Higher State University to its original status as a private institution.

Dean Arnold "Buster" Melvin, PhD, crafted this last sentence for the catalog and lists the accomplishment in his curriculum vitae. "Reach Higher," serves as the dean's mantra for the recent arts and sciences' fund-raising campaign now in its "quiet stages."

CHAPTER 1

August 2004

Nicole Adams' 1992 Volkswagen Jetta had rattled some 150 miles from the Twin Cities to the middle of Iowa. The accumulated assaults of Minnesota winters had finished off most of the car's original paint job, not to mention its chrome trim, and the muffler replacement hung like a wounded animal from the Jetta's underbelly. As the car struggled up the only hill she'd seen since the Minnesota border, Nicole thought about administering last rites.

Despite coughing protests from its overheated engine, and weighed down with Nicole's books, clothes, and boxes, the sagging but resolute Jetta chugged to the crest of the hill. As Nicole turned onto State Highway 42, a cheery red and blue billboard informed her, "Welcome to Normal: Iowa's Happiest City."

"I feel a migraine coming," she informed the Jetta. The car replied with a well-timed mechanical flatulence.

A small state university in the middle of the Midwest would not have been Nicole's first choice to start her academic career. Like most of her graduate student friends in philosophy, she'd hoped for an appointment at a major research university. But the reality of the market for new PhDs in her discipline held no such promise. Nicole had received only the one offer of employment, and that came as a fluke. Still, she looked forward to becoming a college professor.

As she headed down College Avenue toward the campus, Nicole reminded herself how much she wanted to teach at the college level. She wanted to be a damn fine teacher. Her students would share the same excitement and appreciation for learning she had experienced as an undergraduate.

I want to make a difference in their lives, she thought. A good teacher could do that.

Nicole recalled how she had secured her job as an assistant professor. In her final interview, she had met with Arnold "Buster" Melvin, dean of arts and sciences. Why some men insisted on incorporating silly boyhood nicknames in their lives as adult professionals mystified Nicole. Dean Melvin didn't look like a "Buster" at all. He stood barely over five feet five and wore an ill-fitting toupee.

After the usual small talk, Dean Melvin cupped his hands together over his desk and leaned forward with a serious look. "Can you teach a logic course?"

Fortunately, Nicole recalled the job ad in *The Chronicle of Higher Education*. She'd thought it odd at the time, but now the sentence under "Qualifications" made perfect sense. "Ability to teach key areas of the general education curriculum" took on urgent meaning.

Nicole guessed Dean Melvin had no budget left to hire any adjunct professors, and not a single member of the philosophy department would deign to teach the course. Without hesitation, Nicole volunteered to solve the dean's dilemma, and she'd spent much of the past month trying to slap together a course in logic from her undergraduate notes.

At the entry arch leading to the campus, Nicole pulled over to the curb and leaned out the car's window to take a snapshot. Her father had required verification of the university's name.

Two native fieldstone pillars set on either side of the road anchored a soaring arch composed of intricately twisted iron rods. Set into various holes and crannies within the arch, a multitude of metallic decorations sparkled in the late afternoon sun. The effect reminded Nicole of one of those late-sixties, acid-rock album covers her father treasured so much. When she spotted the likenesses of Allen Ginsburg, Timothy Leary, and the Jefferson Airplane clustered together on the right side of the arch—turned out in hammered copper plating and circled with fresh flowers—Nicole accepted the truth of what she had heard about the university's early origins. She assumed the requests for sweatshirts, coffee cups, and knickknacks from her family and friends would be never ending.

Ever since Nicole's job interview, explaining the university's moniker to her friends and family had been a continuing nightmare. Her father kept asking, "So what do they call the football team? . . . the Roaches?"

Dad could be such a stitch. He'd had a ton of suggestions for the fight song. An enormous field of corn stood as a backdrop to the western edge of the campus where Nicole had rented a pale and lonely one-bedroom house. As she hauled her boxes into the sparsely furnished dwelling, she paused on the front porch to take in her surroundings.

An eight-foot-high brick wall loomed to her right enclosing a three-story research laboratory operated by the DeTassell Institute for Organic Farming. Off to the other side, beyond the garage driveway, rows of corn stretched as far as she could see. At perfect intervals in front of every fifth row, which . . . yes . . . "stood high as an elephant's eye," metal signs depicting a yellow ear of corn flying through the air on green wings proclaimed the wonders of "DeKalb Seed Corn." Nicole made plans to steal one of the flying corncob signs for her bedroom.

Once she'd unpacked the car, Nicole collapsed on a sofa in the front room and stared out the picture window. The sky had darkened and filled with stars. Aside from the crickets, all she could hear through the screen door leading outside to the porch was an occasional mechanical hum, signifying the opening and closing of the DeTassell Institute's huge iron gate. What seemed only minutes later, the mawkish chimes of her cell phone jolted Nicole from a deep slumber.

"Are you safe and sound?"

Nicole scrunched back into the cushions of the sofa and reached for the remains of her generic canned cola, now glistening with condensation on the table.

"Are you checking up on me, Dad?"

She could picture her father relaxing in the kitchen at home. Mr. Blifil, the oversized Labrador retriever, would be sprawled on the floor nearby. Her father worked long hours as a supervisor at a printing plant. Her mother had passed away two years ago, a victim of cancer. The nights were a lonely time for her father.

"Do you still think this is the right thing to do? It's not too late to change your mind, you know." Nicole's father had urged her to teach abroad or do some postgraduate work rather than take the Higher State job.

"There'll be other good jobs to come along. You can publish some articles and buff up that résumé." Dad hated the thought of her moving out of Minnesota, though he'd never say so directly.

But Nicole wanted a job. She'd spent most of the past five years living the poor graduate lifestyle, and she had $30,000 worth of student loans to repay. She also worried about the market for philosophers. The predictions about the "Baby Boom generation" retirement and exodus from the profession hadn't proved true. Besides, she wanted to teach and get on with her career.

After a few minutes more on the topic, her father apologized for bringing it up again. "OK. I'll stop. Just consider all the angles."

Scarcely five minutes after talking with her father, the cell phone chimed again. Nicole made a mental note to find a less irritating choice among the twenty-four "ringers" her cell phone contract promised.

The caller turned out to be her major professor, Olaf I. M. Osgood, one of the foremost scholars in the profession. He'd been on a Fulbright exchange to Italy during Nicole's last semester, but sent a full and glowing report accepting her dissertation. His highly praised academic achievements and a crusty personality had most of the grad students running for cover, but he loved Nicole's work.

"Nicole, I urge you to reconsider your acceptance of this assistant professorship." One could never accuse Professor Osgood of dancing around the subject. "You are on the verge of throwing away all the hard work we have put into your graduate education." Nicole didn't quite know what she could say to Professor Osgood to convince him—and herself—that she'd made a good decision.

"I admire your desire to begin your career, and I understand the financial difficulties in which graduate students find themselves. I also regret I was not available to counsel you in regard to the job market. However, I want you to consider these factors."

Nicole felt like she should have a notebook. She knew Osgood meant well, but it didn't make any difference now. She'd signed her contract for the school year with Higher State, and the semester started in a couple of days.

"First," Osgood said, "if you are to persist on this course, understand that you will not be availed of a strong research library to continue your project, and the chances of grants and fellowships from that institution will be few and far between. Second, you'll have a heavy teaching load and an onerous schedule of departmental and university committees."

Nicole walked out to the tiny kitchen in search of a teapot. She figured Osgood was good for at least a ten-minute dissertation on the subject. When she switched off the flame under the teapot before it whistled, her esteemed professor had ticked off an impressive number of strong objections to her job choice. As she dunked an orange pekoe teabag into her cup of hot water, Osgood concluded his litany.

"Finally, Ms. Adams, when it comes to applying for national fellowships and grants, referees will rarely consider applications from young scholars at places the likes of . . . what is the name of that place?"

"Higher State University, sir." Nicole blushed at having to say it.

"Yes . . . well." Osgood fell silent momentarily. "Here's what I propose." Nicole put down her tea and sat cross-legged on the floor. She noticed the yellow-green shag carpeting for the first time.

Osgood continued, "I can arrange a part-time lectureship here at the university and some grading in the undergraduate survey. That way you can work on your publications and search for an appropriate position. I'll be around all year, and I have a number of colleagues in the profession who'd be happy to consider one of my students." Nicole wanted to ask Osgood if those colleagues could manufacture academic positions. It sounded like Nicole's job choice had become an embarrassment. On the other hand, he did call and offer her alternatives. But were they realistic?

After Osgood hung up, Nicole wandered out the front door and sat on the porch swing. She twisted her shoulder-length, auburn hair through her fingers and thought how nice it would be to start chewing her nails again, despite her resolution to the contrary. Something brushed against her bare ankle and she bolted out of the swing. A scraggly black-and-white kitten bounded off the porch and dashed across the lawn toward the DeTassell Institute's brick wall. It disappeared behind a large lilac bush.

"Here, kitty." Nicole followed the route of the kitten's escape.

Behind the lilac bush, she discovered a small opening in the bricks, protected by some rusty strands of barbed wire. Machine noises sounded in the distance, and she could smell something wonderful baking. She guessed the institute must have a cafeteria with freshly baked goods. No telling where the opening led. She made a mental note to investigate in the daylight.

Nicole lingered on the porch before going to bed, hoping the kitten would return. The gentle motion of the porch swing soon lulled her to the edge of sleep, but disquieting notions raised by Professor Osgood and her father still played about the edges of her mind. Had she made the right decision about her career? She wasn't quite sure.

CHAPTER 2

Nicole should have been in front of her Monday 10:00 a.m. Introduction to Logic class in DeTassell Hall. Instead, she'd ended up passing out her syllabus and introducing herself to a room full of students in Robert Hall, only to be interrupted a few minutes after the hour by Carla Unng of the psychology department.

Carla tapped Nicole on the shoulder and whispered, "This particular class of mine is probably more interested in the inability to think logically. I'm afraid you're in the wrong classroom."

After treating Carla to a brief, but fervent apology, Nicole dashed out the door and across the mall. But by the time she arrived at the right classroom, only one student remained.

"Yeah. The rest of them left after ten minutes, but I knew you had a PhD, so I waited the whole fifteen." The young man standing near the podium squared his shoulders. "I'm Ted. I want to major in philosophy."

Ted appraised Nicole like some exotic animal in the zoo. "So you're a philosopher, huh?"

"Yes, that's right." Nicole struggled to ignore the quotation in white script across Ted's blue T-shirt. It read: "How do Philosophers do it?"

Apparently satisfied to know Nicole was the real deal, Ted said he'd see her at the next class meeting. She couldn't help but laugh when she saw the back of his T-shirt as he walked out the door. She hadn't expected that particular philosophical twist.

"Please don't be a philosophy major, Ted," she whispered, hoping he had only the one T-shirt.

The day after Professor Osgood's call, Nicole wasted an entire morning making up excuses she could give to Dean Melvin in order to wriggle out of her contract. In the end, she couldn't rationalize breaking her word and being so unprofessional as to leave the university as fall classes started. She also feared Dean Melvin would literally blow his stack, and imagining the little man's rage scared her. She had this vision of his toupee blasting off his head like a space rocket. Besides, she wanted to get started as a college professor. Always looming, of course, was the need to pay off her college loans. She needed to make some money.

At the office she shared with Professor R. Reynolds Raskin, Nicole half listened to the older man's reminiscences of his early years at the university. Apparently, he had been connected with the DeTassell group before they moved from San Francisco. "Damn shame they still let Jimmy DeTassell and his gang have anything to say about the school. What a scoundrel."

At least this line of conversation was better than Raskin's mumbling about "spies" the day before when Nicole had moved in her books and papers. He made it obvious he took no pleasure in having anyone share his office—particularly anyone of the "female variety."

Dean Melvin had forced the office-sharing issue with Raskin, and as Nicole learned from the department secretary, Melvin and Raskin had been feuding for decades. Raskin allowed Nicole to occupy a small, distant corner of the spacious office. She sat at a wooden desk with barely enough surface to accommodate her computer and a stack of file bins. Much to Raskin's displeasure, Nicole had appropriated an aging file cabinet and a three-shelf bookcase from the building storage room.

"So let me offer a bit of advice if you don't mind." Nicole could barely make Raskin out across the expanse of the office from her tiny corner to where he perched behind his massive desk. "In this academic market, you have to think ahead. Chances are you'll never get another job."

After a brief phone call confirming an upcoming handball game, Raskin turned back to Nicole. "As I was saying, Ms. Adams, since you have this one shot at tenure, you need to make a choice about the Holy Trinity of teaching, publication, and service."

Raskin smoothed an imaginary wrinkle from his blue and gold rep tie. He was a sharp dresser, and looked quite fit despite his years.

"Personally, I prefer granting tenure to folks who can publish," said Raskin. "Teaching is an art. No one knows how to measure good teaching, so you can always dispute any negative findings."

"What about service?" Nicole had only a sketchy idea about that category for tenure decisions.

Raskin waved off her question and spun back to the papers strewn on his desk. He mumbled softly, but loud enough for Nicole to hear, "You'll be well *serviced* in the next few years, believe you me."

"Excuse me," said Nicole. The old buzzard belonged back in the 1950s, yukking it up in the men's locker room.

Raskin turned slightly in his chair, eyeing Nicole under craggy brows. "Don't get your knickers in a knot. It's simple. As a junior member of the department, you'll get all the crummy committee assignments. It's always been that way." He gave her a creepy smile. "That's why tenure is so treasured in academe."

Nicole wondered how many women had been hired or ever received tenure in Raskin's heyday. She already had a good idea. Only one woman's name—a half-time lecturer—appeared on the philosophy department directory outside the office door. Nicole figured tenure would be a long, hard climb.

"I should probably let you find out for yourself what it's like to work in a place like this." Raskin drew a large volume from the bookcase against the wall behind him—something about the marketplace of modern art. Judging from the titles in his bookcase, he seemed to have quite an interest in art.

"I'm not long for any more of this academic life." Raskin marked a page in the art book he now studied.

"What do you mean?" Nicole wished he would make good on his statement sooner than later.

"After thirty-plus years of declining student intelligence, fumbling administrators, brain-challenged colleagues . . . not to mention the feeble amount of money I get paid to put up with all of this—" Raskin's phone rang, and he dismissed their conversation.

"The hell you say!" Raskin thumped his fist on the desktop.

Nicole busied herself sorting through a stack of university memos and forms. She didn't particularly want to hear more of Raskin's complaints, and getting on the wrong side of this guy wouldn't be pleasant.

"You damn fool." Raskin slammed the phone down. He bolted past Nicole's desk and out the office door.

After her noon ethics class, Nicole ate lunch alone at her desk.

Raskin had not returned to teach his classes. Sharing an office with the old coot made her squirm. And what was it with the padlocked steel closet door on the far wall beyond Raskin's desk? He'd been very territorial about the closet when Nicole asked him where the door led.

She spent the rest of the afternoon carefully outlining and writing up lectures for her courses—many in PowerPoint. Next semester will be so much easier, she thought. I'll only have to plug in the dead spots and work in more of the theoretical positions. She hoped her diligence and preparation would impress the department's decision makers.

She brooded a bit on the fact that so far none of her colleagues had come forward to offer her any encouragement or advice. They seemed so friendly when she interviewed for the position. Now that school had started, only a few bid her a brief hello before scurrying off to their classes. Most of the faculty taught in the morning and left the campus or escaped to their library carrels as soon as they could.

I'll show 'em, though. The student evaluations Nicole expected at the end of the semester would open some eyes. Her students would get plenty of information, and they'd have their facts straight. She typed in another PowerPoint slide.

Late in the afternoon, Nicole shut down her computer and collected books and papers for her briefcase. She could eat a quick dinner at the campus center and head home to work on her article for the *Journal of Philosophy Perplexus*. She wondered if her project, "Aristotle's Sandals:

Philosophical Tramps and Ethical Stance" would have any relevance for her students. Was it a better idea to cast her research so it would translate directly into her teaching of undergraduates? Despite her doubts, she squeezed the research notes into her briefcase.

Much of her resolve for the evening stemmed from the fact that she'd fallen asleep watching a stupid reality show on TV the night before. If she didn't buckle down, the research agenda she'd set would never get off the ground. Sometimes she wondered how the philosophy department could expect research and publication in the face of teaching four courses a semester. There seemed to be no balance point.

She also felt an ethical conflict . . . or at least a conflict of values. She wanted most of all to be a good teacher. Her research and writing did border on the esoteric side of philosophy (*Was that an oxymoron?*), so the idea that the likes of "Ted the T-shirt Boy" would benefit from her postmodern approach to philosophy as a discipline, in addition to the obscure terminology she now used with such facility, seemed most unlikely. Would Ted ever experience a "nodal coalescence"? Maybe he had the T-shirt.

Walking through the parking lot to her car, she also felt a nagging sense of isolation. She longed for the camaraderie of her grad school friends, tossing down a beer or two at the local campus hangout after seminars. Higher State didn't offer much charm as a campus, either. Architecturally, with the exception of her office building and a classroom complex, the university seemed more like an office mall than anything else. She felt her isolation accelerating toward alienation.

"Hello Dr. Adams." The voice from behind her scared the hell out of Nicole.

"I'm so sorry . . . did I surprise you?"

Dean Melvin walked around to the front of Nicole's car. A tall woman dressed from head to toe in black and with abundant blonde hair accompanied him. Startled, Nicole knelt beside the Jetta's door, fishing for the car keys she'd dropped in her fright. "Did you lose something, dear?" The shadow woman's perfume drifted down in a heavy cloud.

Nicole held up the keys she'd found by the Jetta's front wheel.

"You really scared me." Nicole smiled a greeting to the woman.

"Oh, I'm so sorry. We must have given you such a fright." The woman extended her hand. "I'm Aurelia Castle . . . Dean Melvin's assistant."

"Pleased to meet you." To Nicole, this woman didn't seem like someone who took orders from the likes of Dean Melvin.

"Are you settling in? Ready for a bang-up semester?" The dean stood next to Aurelia, his hand resting casually on her shoulder. She looked quite a bit younger than at first glance and much more stunning. Nicole had an awful, fleeting vision of the pair locked in a passionate embrace, with Dean Melvin smothered by Aurelia's ample bosom.

"Yes, I think I'll be ready." Nicole tried not to notice as Dean Melvin brushed his fingers over Aurelia's hip.

"Well, you better get home and rest up for tomorrow," said Dean Melvin. "Unfortunately, we still have work to finish."

"No rest for the wicked," Aurelia gave Nicole a wink.

Aurelia and the dean walked toward the darkened administration building, which loomed above the parking lot. Nicole watched their retreat into the distance, wondering what could possibly require their attention so late. She tried to keep her imagination under control, as the images curling through her mind were most likely misbegotten— or, guaranteed to spoil a good night's sleep.

CHAPTER 3

The following morning, Nicole pulled in to the faculty parking lot trailing behind a late-model, red Acura—its oversized tires squealing on the new asphalt surface. Only one spot remained open despite the early hour, and Nicole lost out. She saw no evidence on the Acura's bumper of the required red and blue "HSU Faculty Parking Permit" for the lot.

A young woman emerged from the car, locking it with a casual "bleep" from the remote key she held. Dressed in jeans and a low-cut yellow top, she laid her book bag on the Acura's roof and took a long drink of bottled water.

"Do you know this parking lot is reserved for faculty?" Nicole had maneuvered the Jetta to block the blonde's path.

"Oh bag it, lady. I'm not going to pay twenty-five bucks for parking and then walk all that way to class." The blonde tucked her water bottle into a special slot on her book bag and flounced by Nicole. "God, where did you get that car?"

"Got any books in that bag?" Nicole called out—too late for any effect.

Five minutes later, Nicole found a parking space on a crowded neighborhood street. She jogged almost three blocks to reach her building, and arrived at the entrance out of breath, sweat building on her neck and shoulders. The elevator to the third floor was packed to capacity, so she raced up the stairs. Arriving in the reception area of the philosophy department, she observed several faculty milling about in front of her office.

What now? thought Nicole.

As she cut past a couple of department members, she saw Dean Melvin, Aurelia Castle, and a tall man dressed in a brown suit, light-green shirt, and a perfectly horrid paisley tie walking out of Nicole's office.

"I wouldn't go in there." Felton Bernswaggle, the department's graduate student advisor, steered Nicole toward the coffee station.

"But I've got to get ready for class."

"No can do," Bernswaggle told her in a low whisper. "It's a crime scene."

"What?"

Bernswaggle reported what had taken place, gasping for a quick breath at the end of each sentence, his pudgy cheeks reddened with excitement. According to what he knew, the night janitor put in an emergency call to the campus police after discovering Raskin's office unlocked and his desk and files ransacked.

"They tried to bust into Raskin's office closet, but he'd installed a new set of locks."

Nicole poured herself a cup of coffee, adding a couple of sugar cubes to cut the taste. The department used some generic brand. She'd learned to be a real snob about coffee in grad school.

Bernswaggle pulled impatiently on Nicole's sleeve.

"And guess what?"

"There's more?" Nicole worried how she could teach her class without her folder of notes.

"We've been calling Raskin at home to let him know about the break-in."

"And?"

"He hasn't been there."

"Nicole." Aurelia had detached herself from the conversation with

Dean Melvin and the guy in the brown suit. "I'm afraid you have only a few minutes to gather up what you'll need for teaching this morning. I'm so sorry for the inconvenience, but the police need to take some fingerprint evidence."

Nicole brushed past Aurelia into the office. She threw everything she thought she'd need into the briefcase she carried, squishing her tuna sandwich and Ritz crackers in the bargain. On the floor near a corner of her desk, she noticed some sort of gold pin or charm sparkling in a sliver of morning sunlight. She kneeled down to pick it up.

"I don't think you'd better touch that." Aurelia moved next to Nicole, placing a high-heeled shoe over the object. "It could be evidence, dear. You run off to classes. I'm sure your office space will be free by the time you finish."

Aurelia stood back and appraised Nicole's outfit—a simple black jumper over a white, long-sleeved turtleneck and black tights. "You look . . . very professional. Good luck with your classes."

The students in first-hour Introduction to Ethics had spread themselves throughout the large room assigned for the class. Except for a few bold souls, the front rows of the classroom remained vacant. The bulk of students preferred to sit at the sides and back of the room. A sizable group of "hat-backward boys," as one of Nicole's grad school friends had labeled them, lounged in a corner, trading smirks and whispered asides as Nicole walked toward the teaching station.

Oh, for cripes sake, thought Nicole, it's an electronic classroom. I bet they'll expect me to use every one of those gizmos. At least she had mastered PowerPoint.

The size and bulk of the teaching station took up a good share of the available room in front of the class, and standing behind it, Nicole felt like a knight behind a castle wall.

She made her way to the first row and posed near one of the desks.

"Welcome to Philosophy 221: Ethics. We'll start today going through the course syllabus." As she walked across the front of the room, Nicole could hear some snickers coming from behind her. She resolved not to notice.

After distributing the syllabus, Nicole gave her students a few minutes to glance through the document. She'd spent a great deal of time and effort to make it comprehensive, thinking her efforts would signal to students how much she cared about teaching a good course.

"How are you going to grade us?" asked a woman, who looked like she might be a few years older than the other students.

"Let me call the class roll before I answer that question." Nicole smiled and pulled out the computer listing of students from one of her folders.

As Nicole understood from a recent administrative memo, the Financial Aid Office needed attendance records from the first day of class. Apparently, too many students had been claiming financial aid checks without completing classes.

She went through the list of forty students. All of them had shown up for the first day of class. Learning their names would be difficult, but Nicole figured she'd have time to do that. Besides, some of the students would probably drop the class once they read the syllabus carefully. She'd set a full agenda of exams and a required library research paper.

After calling the roll of students and carefully checking off those present for the class, Nicole shuffled through her other folders to find her copy of the syllabus. She spent the next ten minutes reading through its various sections. Most of the students stared back at her with vacant expressions, not bothering to take any notes. Two students in the back of the room had fallen sound asleep, their heads lolling sideways. The sight of the two sleepers infuriated Nicole. She couldn't for the life of her remember the students' names from calling the class roll.

Determined not to let anything disrupt the first meeting of the ethics class, Nicole cut short the reading of the syllabus and glanced over at the woman who'd asked her about grading. Nicole smiled in her direction. "Now I can answer your question."

Most of the students looked at her with more interest than they'd shown before. On cue, the two sleeping students awoke, their eyes glazed and unfocused.

Nicole said, "I think if you will read the second page of the syllabus, you'll see all the assignments and tests spelled out in detail, along with some hints about what it takes to get a good grade in my class."

"Let me warn you. If I catch anyone plagiarizing material, the penalties will be swift and strong." Nicole put on her most serious expression—the one her father used when she was a teenager.

She hated plagiarism with a passion. As a graduate assistant, she'd read too many papers from lazy students who'd copied something off the Internet word for word. As she looked around the room, most of the students had their eyes cast down, scanning the syllabus. A few looked alarmed and confused. Mission accomplished, Nicole thought to herself.

By the sounds in the hall, quite a few professors had dismissed their classes early. Nicole had prepared a simple group discussion exercise for the first class. She wanted to introduce students to the same excitement she'd experienced in her introductory ethics course. It had been a learning experience she'd never forgotten.

Nicole explained what she expected in the group exercise, and asked the students to quickly move their desks around and form into groups of five. After a few minutes of grousing, loud talk between friends, and one section of male students playing bumper cars with their desks, Nicole called a halt to the mayhem. She spent the next five minutes establishing groups and refereeing the movement of desks.

"Now that we have finally accomplished what seems to me the simplest of tasks, here's the situation I want you to discuss. Please listen to the case carefully and take some notes to guide your discussions. I'll want each group to come up with a consensus answer and report it to the class."

Nicole thought the students would really enjoy discussing the simple case she had in mind. "You are in the middle of downloading some of the best cuts off of the most recent Panda Dave and the Moving Vowels CD, *Son of the Red-Headed Stepson . . . Live!* All of a sudden, a message flashes on the screen warning that it's illegal to download this album. It's a school computer and Internet hookup, and you've seen your roommates downloading music off the same site. Would it be wrong for you to continue downloading the music? Is this a situation calling for ethical decision making? If so, why? If not, why not?"

Nicole looked up from reading. Her students stared back at her.

"OK. You can go ahead and discuss the case now," Nicole said.

None of the groups seemed the slightest bit interested in beginning. Did they need more instructions? She overheard one of the students whisper, "That Panda Dave album reeks anyway."

Nicole sat at the console desk fiddling with the computer, waiting to see what conversations the groups might attempt. It didn't take long for the majority of the students to start joking around and talking about anything but the case study. Several students glanced at the clock. Only ten minutes remained in the period. The students busied themselves by packing up their books, and a rising chorus of backpack zippers rose throughout the room.

The whole exercise had been a colossal failure.

Nicole felt defeated, and she had looked forward to teaching the ethics class. She couldn't bear the thought of debriefing each group. She'd heard no substantive discussion from any corner of the room.

"Since this is the first day of classes, and I'm sure you need some time to read the syllabus and get organized, let's cut class short today." Nicole tried not to sound defeated.

"Yeah. That's the spirit!" One of the hat-backward boys smiled brightly at Nicole. He uncoiled his long legs and stood up. The rest of the class readied to leave the classroom.

Nicole shouted above the din of talk and laughter. "I'll expect a one-paragraph analysis of today's case at the next class session."

Her announcement seemed to have little effect as the students crowded toward the door. Nicole retreated behind the dock of electronic classroom equipment as the students rushed from the room.

The older woman who'd asked the question about grades hesitated, but walked past Nicole, trailing the other students to the hall.

Late that night, sitting on the porch swing in the moonlight, nibbling on a tin of crackers her sister had sent from Harrods in London, Nicole thought about the classes she had taught during the day. Despite all her preparations, neither of her ethics sections had gone well. She couldn't help but think some of the problem rested with her teaching. She gave herself a mental slap on the wrist for being negative toward her students and not pushing to reach them—no matter how uninterested and resistant many appeared to be.

She needed to know more about her students. How could she find out about them? Why were most of them going to school anyway? What sorts of ethical situations might they recognize from their own experience? Why didn't they like Panda Dave's music?

Good questions, thought Nicole, and she went inside to read the day's edition of the *Normal News Register* she'd found in her mail slot as a subscription promotion.

She knew little about the town and what if any stores and entertainment it offered. The front page of the newspaper featured an article on a former Higher State University faculty member, Lazlo O'Callaghan. The headline read "Former HSU Artist's Work Earns Hefty Payoff." Nicole scanned the first paragraph and learned O'Callaghan was a multitalented painter, sculptor, architect, and performance artist who had been among the founding members of the university.

A soft mewing from the porch broke Nicole's concentration.

"Here, kitty cat. Want a treat?" Nicole crumbled one of the crackers and tossed the pieces on the floorboards. The kitten made no movement.

"They're from Harrods."

The kitten rose on its tiptoes and curled into a fine stretch, its tail an inverted U. It advanced in slow but regal steps to sniff the cracker crumbs. Satisfied of the cracker's gourmet worthiness, the kitten sampled the treat with dainty bites. When Nicole reached out to pick up the black-and-white ball of fluff, her visitor scurried off to a safe distance by the porch steps. There it remained, licking its paws, staring warily in the direction of its hostess, and every so often mewing in forlorn tones. When Nicole placed more cracker bits on the floor, the kitten threw caution to the wind and bounded over to eat. After consuming the crumbled crackers, it jumped up next to Nicole, snuggled against her leg and fell asleep purring like a finely tuned sports car.

"Maybe you'll show me where you live tomorrow." Nicole thought about the opening in the fence surrounding the Institute for Organic Farming. She wondered what went on behind those walls.

"Do you think they're grinding up poor Professor Raskin into fertilizer, kitty?"

CHAPTER 4

Three weeks had passed since Professor Raskin had failed to show up at his office. His mysterious disappearance baffled campus and city police. Members of the philosophy department's coffee klatch continued to speculate about the missing professor's fate, but Nicole had precious little time to think about anything except preparing and teaching her classes. Every so often, though, as she munched a quick snack in her office in the late afternoon, she permitted herself to wonder what had happened to her obnoxious colleague. Maybe she should be afraid for herself?

That was ridiculous. She hadn't been around long enough to make those sorts of enemies. Not so Professor Raskin, who probably had a whole sackful collected over a lengthy career.

As Nicole polished off the rest of her peanut butter and jelly sandwich, the phone buzzed ominously on Raskin's desk. She scurried across the room and picked up the receiver. At 3:30 on a Friday afternoon everybody had left the department offices—no one around to second-guess her decision to answer the phone.

"Professor Raskin's office." Nicole did a pretty good imitation of the department secretary's nasal greeting, especially with peanut butter still clamped on her molars.

"Who the hell is this?" The voice sounded suspiciously like some-one who had watched too many 1930s gangster movies. "Listen, babe, and listen careful."

"Just spill the beans." Nicole had watched her share of old movies, too. Who was this idiot?

"Is this the gal professor?"

Obviously the caller was lost in the same time warp as Professor Raskin. Nicole reluctantly decided to play along.

"What do you want?" Nicole sat in Raskin's comfy office chair.

"If you want the old guy back safe and sound, get out of the office building now. I'll be watching to see you walking out the front door and heading to the library. Check out a book . . . read one of them stupid-ass women's lib magazines. But don't come back for one hour."

"You've got to be kidding." Nicole looked out the office window. Maybe the caller was somewhere on the campus mall with a cell phone.

"You've got two minutes to make it out the door. Move it . . . that is, if you want Raskin back in one piece." Nicole fought back the urge to tell this creep she couldn't care less if Raskin came back filleted like a sashimi tuna.

"Come on . . . This is so lame," she said, leaning out over the window transom for a wider view of the mall.

"A minute forty seconds, babe—"

Nicole slammed down the phone and gathered up her purse and briefcase. On her way out, she locked her office door and the main door for the department.

"He didn't say anything about leaving things open," she said to the empty hallway.

Once she'd double-timed it across the mall to the library, Nicole figured she could call the campus police. The minute she entered the library, she raced for the circulation desk to use the phone.

"Nicole . . . you look like you've just seen a ghost. What on earth is wrong?" Dean Melvin grasped her elbow, directing Nicole away from a student arguing with a library assistant about checking out vintage issues of *National Geographic*.

Nicole quickly told the dean about the phone threat. "Can you call the campus police? They may be able to catch whoever called."

"Of course, Nicole. You sit down and I'll be right back." Dean Melvin pointed her to one of the comfy reading sofas where students slept between classes. As Nicole sat down, she noticed what looked like dried drool on one of the pillows. She moved over to sit at a table piled high with dictionaries and a large thesaurus.

Dean Melvin had charged into the head librarian's office to use the phone. After a couple of minutes, he returned, pulling up a chair next to Nicole.

"I've called the campus police, and they're on the way. I doubt they'll be able to do much." Dean Melvin patted Nicole's hand. She tried not to cringe.

"I'll take things from here with the authorities," Dean Melvin cooed.

Nicole wanted to slam an *Oxford English Dictionary* on the hand patting her arm. She got up from the desk chair instead so that she towered above the dean.

"If you have everything under control then, I'll head home," said Nicole.

"Splendid idea. But allow me a minute more of your precious time."

"What is it?" Nicole struggled to keep the irritation from her voice. "I have a bunch of papers to grade."

Dean Melvin stroked the dorky little goatee he'd acquired since she'd last seen him and gave her his best administrator's smile. Nicole assumed that college administrators, like the local TV-news personalities, attended special seminars to perfect things like that.

"I want you to take on an important committee assignment, Nicole."

Dean Melvin pulled out a folded sheet of paper from within his suit jacket. Nicole noticed the gold Phi Beta Kappa pin he wore on his lapel. It was like the one she'd seen on her office floor.

"Despite the fact you are our newest faculty member, I think you bring some special qualities I'd like to . . . ummm . . . *exploit* for the betterment of our educational thrust at this institution."

Nicole wondered how she could be exploited any more than she already felt around the dean.

"You bring a fresh perspective to the teaching and learning process." Dean Melvin primped up the silk handkerchief peeking out of the breast pocket of his suit jacket. "I want you to be a member of our

'Push the Pedagogy' faculty team. It's part of a grant I originated with
the DeTassell Foundation. They have been very generous. Sometimes
I wonder how they can afford such largesse. Anyway, there'll be a nice
stipend for your service on the committee and a chance for a special
faculty fellowship over the summer."

Dean Melvin's eyes danced with excitement. He cocked his head
from side to side like a metronome, anticipating Nicole's answer. What
was this? *Jeopardy*?

Leaning forward, hands clasped together under his chin, the trace
of a smile playing across his lips, Dean Melvin continued in a confi-
dential tone. "It's an extra $2,000 a semester, and the summer fellow-
ship is $5,000. You can have a check for this semester's $2,000 stipend
immediately. What's to think about?"

Nicole envisioned $2,000 added on to the present puny balance of
her checkbook. "What do I have to do?"

The next day, Nicole found a large manila envelope marked "Personal
and Urgent" in her faculty mailbox. The official-looking memo ap-
pointed Nicole to the "Push the Pedagogy" team. It also contained a
schedule of team meetings and "classroom visits." Nicole saw her name
next to Professor Bob Olufssen's Introduction to Spanish course from
1:30 to 2:30 p.m. Dean Melvin had penned a short message in the margin.

"Sorry about throwing you into the frying pan so quickly," the dean
had written. "Enclosed is the reporting form our committee uses."

Despite Nicole's anxiety about the committee assignment, a little part
of her looked forward to her role. Besides, she'd overheard quite a bit
about Professor Olufssen from student conversation. He'd captured the
hearts, if not the minds, of most women undergraduates at the school.
Enrollments in Spanish had surged since he joined the faculty. As one of
the women graduate students in philosophy had blurted out to a friend
at the coffee machine, "He can conjugate my verbs anytime he'd like."

At 1:25, Nicole met fellow committee member Paula Pendergrass
outside Olufssen's classroom. Paula had taught chemistry at Higher
State for the past ten years before signing on with Dean Melvin as an
assistant dean. A dark-haired beauty with a striking figure, enhanced
by an expensive-looking blue suit, Paula looked ready for a date with

some movie star, rather than an hour with a herd of students struggling to learn a foreign language. Maybe Señor Olufssen might live up to all the hype after all.

Entering the classroom, Nicole and Paula found students enthusiastically talking in small groups seated at round tables. Bob Olufssen shared a laugh with a group of students and waved hello to his visitors.

"Do you speak any Spanish?" asked Bob.

Paula colored slightly, adding to her already beautiful complexion. *"Un poco,"* she giggled in return.

Bob shifted his blue eyes to Nicole, running a hand through ash-blond hair. "I'm Bob Olufssen. Glad to meet you."

"Encantada, Bob." Nicole hoped he wouldn't expect more. It had been a long time since a year of high school Spanish.

Bob favored both women with a wide smile.

He invited his guests to sit at a table with two students. "We have a couple of kids absent today, so you two accomplished linguists can fill in with Rick and Brittany."

As Bob turned away and made his way to the front of the class, Nicole noticed—in spite of herself—the young professor's trim, Levi-encased backside. A barely audible sigh escaped Paula's lips.

"You're supposed to evaluate Bob's class on the basis of these questions, so take notes," she said, handing Nicole a printed list. "Write up your comments later and send it to me in the dean's office."

"Does my evaluation count for anything?" asked Nicole.

Paula scrunched her eyebrows. "What do you mean?"

"Will what I write be used in salary or tenure decisions?"

"It's not supposed to, but I'm not sure if the dean does anything official with these."

"I've never had any training to evaluate another teacher." Nicole felt uneasy now about the whole exercise.

Paula didn't seem concerned. "You'll attend a training seminar later in the semester, and I'm sure Dean Melvin wouldn't take your evaluation seriously now."

The other woman didn't seem to notice the implication of what she'd said, and Nicole felt even worse.

Bob had supplied each table with a neat pile of materials—three-inch-by-five-inch cards with Spanish vocabulary, maps of Seville, exterior shots of several buildings, and a painting by Goya. "As I told you last time, this exercise is on the CD-ROM each of you got from me at the start of the course. It's also on the computers in the language lab. Don't forget, we'll be in the language lab for tomorrow's class."

Bob walked around the room as he set up the exercise. "Your task today is to work in groups of four, communicating with each other in Spanish only, and solving the problem indicated on the direction card."

Without even a "let's begin" from their instructor, the groups at each table jumped to their task. The room buzzed with students speaking in rudimentary Spanish and helping each other with pronunciation and vocabulary. Bob quietly joined groups and answered questions or observed the discussions. After fifteen minutes of activity, he rapped on a table. The students seemed to expect Bob's signal, and within a few seconds, the classroom noise had stopped. Nicole couldn't believe it. Her students wouldn't do the same for her.

"OK. Let's ask tables four and seven to report on any problems up to this point," said Bob.

A student from each of the tables took a minute to report. Bob asked for a show of hands from the other tables if they were having the same problems. "This week's group reporters need to give me a listing of the two main problems facing your group today. There's a reporting sheet for that among your materials."

Bob stood next to Nicole and Paula. In a conspiratorial tone, Bob told his students that Nicole and Paula had completed at least a year of Spanish. "So, do you guys want to have a race with these language pros to see if they can beat you finishing up the exercise?"

All but a few students raised their hands in favor of the challenge.

"Are the rest of you OK with majority rules on this one?" asked Bob. The students who'd not raised their hands seemed unperturbed by the prospect of joining the others in the competition. Bob smiled and told the class to resume the exercise.

The next twenty minutes went quickly, and just as Nicole and Paula's group neared a solution to the problem, students at a nearby table called Bob over to check their answer. After a minute of checking their solution, he gave a thumbs-up signal to the rest of the room.

"Thanks to all the groups for working diligently on the activity and doing so well on a difficult assignment." Bob stood at the winning table, his hands resting on the shoulders of two group members. "We have about ten minutes left in the class period, and I'd like to use that time for a couple of things."

"He seems like quite a teacher," Nicole whispered to Paula.

Paula winked at Nicole. "I'm not so sure about all this 'touchy-feely' teaching, but I'll give him high marks for 'presentation.'"

Nicole didn't feel comfortable playing the "If you know what I mean" game, but she gave Paula a smile in return. Nicole wanted to see what the handsome young Spanish teacher would do with the remaining time.

For the next five minutes, Bob asked his students to reflect on the day's activity, asking things like, "What was the most difficult thing about what we did today? How did yesterday's session on idioms help you? What seemed to be the biggest stumbling block you had speaking today?"

Most of the students seemed at ease in contributing answers, and few of their responses seemed phony or self-promoting. The majority of the students wanted Bob to favor them with one of his smiles or a congratulatory remark.

"I'd like all of you to fill out a couple of sentences for this question," Bob passed around half sheets of paper.

The class busied themselves writing answers. Bob handed Paula and Nicole copies of the question: "How could you apply today's learning to a situation you might meet outside this classroom?"

Nicole stared at her question sheet, wondering how the students might respond. She caught Brittany looking at her, obviously upset about something.

"I think this is yours." Brittany shoved her sheet across the table and took Nicole's. She removed her funky reading glasses and adjusted her chair so that she faced toward the front of the classroom.

Nicole looked at the question sheet, and she understood Brittany's behavior. Bob had written across the bottom, "How about a late lunch after class?"

Nicole didn't know what to think, and busied herself with the multicopy "Push the Pedagogy" form.

CHAPTER 5

Bob Olufssen proved a far more complicated and interesting date than Nicole had imagined. Instead of a quick bite at Kampus Kuizine—a horrendous gastronomic experience even for undergraduates—Bob had whisked Nicole into his silver BMW two-seater and raced to the one decent restaurant in Normal.

Noodles and Nice offered a selection of French-Asian fusion dishes and, according to local connoisseurs, served the best martini outside of Des Moines (which Nicole did not take to be a five-star recommendation, especially when she glimpsed Ted, the would-be philosophy major, behind the bar mixing drinks). The restaurant's hostess, a stylish redhead in her midthirties, escorted the couple to a remote booth and gave Bob a conspiratorial wink before gliding off to fetch the wine list.

"We must celebrate this occasion with a bottle of wine." Bob donned a pair of half reading glasses and tilted his head back slightly to read the wine list. "They have a wonderful New Zealand Sauvignon Blanc. Let's have that with bread and cheese since it's so late in the afternoon."

Nicole agreed with Bob's choices, all the while thinking how irresistible he looked with those cute little glasses. His perfectly cut, gray herringbone sport jacket worn over a slate blue Ralph Lauren broadcloth shirt was not standard issue at "Buddy's Men's Wear" in the West Normal Mall. Her dining partner had a "complexity," Nicole concluded, like the wine she sipped. He also had more money than the average associate professor.

"How is your wine? It has a whisper of tartness, don't you think?" Bob raised an eyebrow.

"It's definitely naughty," answered Nicole, feeling quite saucy. Après-dinner possibilities fluttered through her mind, although she had only seconds to savor that option.

"I'm so glad I found you two here." Aurelia Castle's statuesque form loomed over the pair.

"The dean's secretary happened to see you dash off campus," said Aurelia, fixing her attention on Bob. "I took the chance you might have headed here. Do you mind if I sit down for a minute? I have important news."

"I guess so." Nicole made room on the bench seat for Aurelia. Instead, Aurelia slid in next to Bob. The pair looked like models for a shampoo add with their luxuriant blond hair.

"The campus police have just left the dean, and they report nothing amiss in your office, Nicole."

"But what about the call warning me to leave?"

"It must have been some crank. Maybe a student, dear."

Aurelia shifted closer to Bob and placed her hand on his arm. "Our students can be so juvenile and reckless sometimes. Isn't that your experience, Bob?"

"I think that's probably true." Bob took a studied drink of his wine. "Aurelia's usually right about these things."

"Thanks for letting me know what you found out." Nicole hoped her words had the tinge of sincerity she didn't feel. "I'm glad it wasn't anything serious."

"Oh, goodness. I almost forgot. The dean wants to ask a big favor, Nicole." Aurelia drew a sheath of official-looking papers from her oversized leather handbag. "You have a class from 8:00 to 9:00 tomorrow don't you?"

"If that's what it says on your schedule." Not the nicest reply, but

Nicole didn't care much how the other woman would react at that moment. Bob buried a smirk in his wine glass.

"Good. The dean wants you to take a reading on how Professor Porter is doing with the students in his literature class. It seems he is the victim of a certain amount of . . . what do they call it, Bob?"

"I think the term is 'student incivility.'"

Bob reached for the wine bottle and poured himself another glass. Nicole sensed a tension between the two dating back some time.

"Thank you. I think that is the description Dean Melvin applied." Aurelia straightened the place setting in front of her. "At any rate, Nicole, it looks as though the newest member of the 'Push the Pedagogy' committee will ride again."

"I don't understand why Dean Melvin would want me to visit this class. I'm no expert on any of this stuff."

"But that's the point, dear." Aurelia consulted the memo again. "The dean wants your fresh point of view. Someone closer to our students' age."

This time, Nicole reached for the wine bottle. She was so mad, she didn't know whether to drink it or throw it after the retreating form of the dean's assistant. Bob watched Aurelia exit with a pained smile on his face.

At 7:55 a.m., Nicole waited outside Professor Augustus Porter's American literature classroom. From what Bob had told her last evening, Porter held a recently endowed chair named for Vern "Thunder Jam" Berkersen, by far the most famous alumnus of Higher State University. Thunder Jam had led the university basketball team to the NCAA regional finals in 1990.

As Bob had explained the evening before, while completing a required Introduction to Literature course, "Thunder Jam" had taken a great liking to Ole Rolvaag's novel *Giants in the Earth*—a story of Norwegian immigrant life on the Dakota prairies in the late nineteenth century. Although he failed to pass the course (having read only Rolvaag's novel), as a farmer's son and a native of Fargo, young "Thunder Jam" had experienced an intense literary connection he would not soon forget.

If you were seven foot one and 260 pounds with a feather-soft hook shot and, of course, a patented "thunder jam," Nicole imagined you could read and like whatever the hell you wanted at Higher State University.

Once Thunder Jam signed his second multimillion-dollar contract with the Chicago Bulls, he gladly funded an endowed chair. Dean Melvin had played an instrumental role in securing the basketball star's support for this inspiring academic legacy—involving, of course, a number of trips to Chicago for the NBA playoffs.

Augustus Porter, then in his late fifties, had accepted the Berkersen Chair of Literature and migrated to Higher State from his tenured professorship at the University of Chicago.

"Why?" Nicole hadn't meant to blurt out her question.

"One hundred twenty thousand dollars a year, a house, a paid research leave every third semester, and he only teaches one class," Bob had informed her.

"That's it?"

"Well, the class he teaches is the required Introduction to Literature for nonmajors—not exactly a plum teaching assignment."

Nicole figured she'd teach that course and whatever else they wanted for $120,000.

"He does have to advise the Norwegian Literature and Ski Club."

"Are there any members?"

"Not that anyone knows about."

What could be the problem? Did someone like Augustus Porter need a classroom intervention? Nicole decided she would forgo meeting the professor before the hour and took a seat in the back corner of his classroom. She could introduce herself after class.

At exactly 8:00 a.m., Professor Porter entered the classroom and paused to survey the students. Some thirty-five seekers of enlightenment populated a room that should have seated thirty. Students unpacked their book bags and gossiped back and forth. Nicole overheard a young woman tell the boy next to her, "Professor Beaker better give me a passing grade in chemistry. My parents are paying a fortune for me to go here, and I've been to every class."

The two students spotted Porter's advance to the lectern and whispered to each other like Roman conspirators on the Ides of March. The professor gave the class a perfunctory greeting, ignored a student raising her hand, and squared his note cards. The student pair continued their discourteous tête-à-tête.

Such rude behavior! Nicole had never thought of acting like that in her student days.

"Please. Please. Will the class come to order so that we can proceed with today's lesson?" Porter avoided looking directly at the two students still engaged in conversation and apparently oblivious to the request for order. A lone adult student in the class "shushed" the offenders. The younger students stared at her as if she were crazy.

As Porter led the class through what should have been a humorous problem-solving topic—"Shakespeare, Pete Rose, and Authorial Signature: Who Should We Trust?"—a student in the third row turned his baseball cap around so that it faced forward. He smirked and lowered the brim well over his beady eyes in what Nicole could only imagine as a significant affront to deconstructive jousting with literary texts. Some students appeared to glare at Porter, as if daring him to teach. Bursts of conversation switched on and off throughout the classroom.

Five minutes later, two young women walked into the room, passing in front of the professor at his lectern. He paused and waited until the students found seats. As they completed their entrance, another student arrived late to class. Porter glared at the offender, who waved at two friends on the far side of the room.

After ten minutes, Porter had advanced well into the substance of his main lecture topic, "The Conflicted Search for Authenticity on Norman Mailer's Feminine Side."

While Nicole didn't quite understand Porter's lecture, she found it interesting nevertheless. He paused every ten minutes to pose general questions to the class, although he rarely received any response other than rather loud, disapproving groans from students in the back of the room. Some students slept covertly; others had no intention of taking notes on the lecture. When a student cell phone rang, Porter slammed his notes down.

"If your damn phone call is more important than giving me your attention in the classroom, don't bother coming."

Porter's eyes searched the room, trying to identify the cell phone owner. He sighed loudly and muttered something under his breath—a sentiment Nicole guessed would cause a lip reader to blush.

Near the end of the hour, to loud cries of displeasure, the professor divided the class into small groups for a brief discussion of what they found "most important" or "most confusing" about the lecture. Two students near the back, undeterred by the previous communications flap, took the occasion to answer messages on cell phones. When it came time for short reports from selected groups, Porter purposely called on the young man and woman near Nicole who'd been among the least attentive. Only two minutes remained in the class period.

"This is stupid and a huge waste of my time," the petite redhead groused, loud enough for Porter to hear. She smiled at her companion, a young man with his hair gelled and odd groups of it standing at attention like haystacks.

"This is busy work," she persisted in her diatribe, "and none of this stuff makes any difference. What's the point?" She fixed Porter with an awful gaze.

"Right on," her friend applauded.

The two students and a considerable number of others in the class glowered at the professor. The bell saved further unpleasantness, and everyone evacuated the room. Porter watched them leave, a look of anguish and bewilderment etched on his face.

CHAPTER 6

TENDE ALTIUS

After finishing her "Push the Pedagogy" report on Professor Porter and teaching her morning classes, Nicole rushed to the science building lecture hall for the semester's first faculty meeting. To her disappointment, she caught a glimpse of Bob Olufssen and Paula Pendergrass entering the hall arm in arm. Paula had on a deep blue matching skirt-and-sweater outfit that drew the rapt attention of several faculty members. Nicole felt a stab of jealousy as the pair sat down together in the far back row.

"Nicole, come sit."

Maddie Sturgis and Ann Speidel, new faculty members in the communications department, waved and pointed to an empty chair. Nicole squeezed past several women she recognized from the presemester orientation session.

"Meet Clark MacKenzie, the history department's rising star." Maddie tapped the broad shoulder of a man sitting immediately in front of her.

Clark McKenzie twisted around as best he could in the tight surroundings and favored Nicole with a pleasant smile. As she settled back, awaiting the meeting's start, Nicole couldn't help but steal a glance at Professor MacKenzie's handsome profile. She'd always liked her history courses.

A woman in a polyester pantsuit well past its prime seized the podium and treated individual faculty members throughout every corner of the auditorium to a withering appraisal.

"All right, people. Let's settle down. I'm not going to ask you children more than once."

Dr. Corinne Runting, head of the economics department and long-term president of the Faculty Association, ignored the laughter of her colleagues and smacked down a file of papers on the podium.

Runting directed the assembled faculty to the meeting agenda, now PowerPointed on the large screen behind her. The meeting would be divided into two parts, with a thirty-minute break for refreshments. Runting quickly superimposed a heading over the schedule—"Crisis at Higher State University."

Talk about an attention grabber. Nicole inched forward in her seat, as did a majority of the faculty.

"I'm going to ask all you 'Robert's Rules of Order' fetishists to cool your jets today," said Runting. "We have things to do and not enough time to spare."

Ignoring a few but fervently raised hands throughout the lecture hall, Runting continued her introductory remarks.

"We've learned student enrollments are down a cataclysmic 15 percent this fall, and this puts us in a very difficult situation. Dean Melvin also informs me that we have overspent on several grant programs and campus projects recommended by our Board of Seers. When you combine this loss of revenue stream with an unexpected screwup on student loan payments," Runting drew a deep breath, "resulting in an estimated payback of two million smackers, we find ourselves in deep financial doo-doo."

Nicole and those around her shifted in their chairs as Runting dashed through other statistics on the financial crisis, including the costs of hiring too many new faculty members.

"How the hell did all this happen?"

The question came from a portly gentleman whose face had turned a florid red from struggles to maintain his balance working his way to the aisle. "This is outrageous."

"Careful, careful, Roger," Runting soothed. "Better sit down before I drop the other shoe."

Over the next ten minutes, the faculty learned of serious questions posed by a regional accrediting association's report that arrived on the heels of a consultant-evaluator team's visit the previous spring. The university could expect a "focused visit" near the end of the school year about finances and assessment.

"The rub is the accrediting association received a well-documented complaint after the consultant-evaluators had pretty much accepted our self-study report."

Runting shook a sizable file at the faculty audience. "In my opinion, thanks to some Judas in our midst, we are close to being placed on probation."

Roger Cantwell of the political science department bolted to the aisle once more, leaning heavily on the shoulder of a woman sitting on the end chair. "Are you telling me all this assessment poppycock has evolved to the point where we are at jeopardy as an institution?"

Cantwell discoursed against "an assessment conspiracy," fomented by a dangerous cabal of "doctorates in education." His voice rose to a squeal and he evinced his aggravation by shaking the poor woman's shoulder he grasped. She had little defense, and resembled a Raggedy Ann doll under Cantwell's grip.

"Roger! Stop this instant," Runting roared. "You'll snap Virginia's damn neck."

Cantwell released the flailing Virginia, and the partners in the odd dance struggled to restore their dignity.

"I demand a discussion period," Cantwell said, fluffing his bow tie back to a proper angle.

"I agree." Runting called for a list of those desiring to speak on the issue and scrawled names on a whiteboard. "No more than five minutes per speaker, people. I am keeping time. Roger, as long as you're still on your feet, you start."

Cantwell needed no prodding and launched into an all-out attack on academic assessment.

To Nicole, assessment seemed the least of the university's problems compared to the financial disaster Runting had described. She worried about losing her job.

Cantwell's attacks on the education department and "its spineless politically correct faculty," left no doubt he had little use for creating a "culture of assessment" at Higher State.

Nicole knew precious little about the assessment issue and she didn't much care for Cantwell's style, but some things he said made an impression.

"Let me count the ways I hate assessment." Cantwell moved to the front of the hall so he could have a full audience. He held up his hand, waggling his fingers at the audience. "I hope I don't run out of digits, but five points should do the job."

"First," Cantwell started his oration, bending his thumb over, "assessment is time taken away from teaching and research, not to mention advising students. Second, we are simply attempting to satisfy external agents and bureaucratic legislative idiots in this state with a flurry of inapplicable, inconsequential mass testing and bogus statistical conclusions. And don't get me started on the misuse of statistics by a bunch of amateurs." Cantwell, now in full rhetorical plumage, strutted stage center, all faculty eyes following him now.

"Third," said Cantwell, "assessment at this university and elsewhere generally demonstrates no trust in our skills and learning as professors. It's insulting. Fourth, you ask a bunch of students into a mass test that has no relationship to their classes here at Higher State and I'll guarantee they won't participate. And if they do, I'd hope these students would finish quick and get the hell out of the testing room. Standardized, mass testing tells us nothing useful about how we are teaching our students here at Higher State."

Like members of the British House of Lords, several faculty grunted their agreement. Cantwell soaked up the encouragement, pulling down his remaining finger. "Fifth, this bane of academic life in the twenty-first century threatens how I wish to conduct my teaching and what I consider important for students to learn. I will not teach to some outside test. My liberal friends on the faculty, always on the lookout for noble causes, should consider joining me for this one. I consider it a potential fight for academic freedom—especially if some on our campus are successful in establishing their plan of local, classroom-based assessment."

Examining his closed fist, Cantwell smiled. "I rest my case for the moment, though I could continue." Raising his fist and shaking it above his head, he shouted, "To the barricades!"

The majority of faculty erupted in applause and cheers as Cantwell returned to his aisle. As she assessed the cheering throng, Nicole wished she had paid more attention at new-faculty orientation when the assessment coordinator explained the university's plan.

Maddie leaned over and whispered, "What he didn't add is we already give grades. That's assessment in my book."

But Nicole recalled the assessment coordinator had argued against grading being used as assessment. What did she say? Something about grades not being tied to "specific learning outcomes." Or was it the other way around?

As Cantwell paraded to his seat, mugging for his supporters, Alice Diugud, professor of mathematics and chair of the Assessment Committee, moved to the front of the room. A petite woman with a pleasant smile, Diugud spoke so softly that Corinne Runting had to shout for order.

"'To the barricades,' Roger? Mon Dieu!" Diugud fluttered her fingers near her lips. "This issue must have touched you deeply in your soul. Does this mean you'll be selling your Nixon-Agnew campaign buttons?"

This could be good, thought Nicole. No fragile flower was Alice. "Let's get real, shall we?" Diugud adjusted the cuffs of her crisply ironed pink blouse. "If faculty do not take hold of this assessment task, someone else will. Do those who cheered for Roger want state legislators and bureaucrats messing with our academic business? Do you want some administrative center staffed by nonteachers measuring the quality of our academic enterprise at Higher State?"

A reluctant murmur of noes answered Diugud's questions, and she followed up her successful opening gambit with more.

"Do you think we can ignore the accreditation and legislative mandates for accountability? Why shouldn't parents and students have specific, reliable information that speaks to academic outcomes? Shouldn't we be ready with evidence about the quality of our teaching and how well our students learn?"

These questions brought a mixed response from the faculty.

"Why don't we find some national, standardized tests and require students to take them for graduation?" asked one of the faculty members near the back. Roger Cantwell turned around to glare at the speaker.

A chorus of questions rained down from all sides of the room: "What are these academic outcomes?" "What's 'value added' all about?" "What sort of educational jargon are we going to have to learn for all this?"

Alice Diugud folded her arms across her chest and waited patiently until the faculty quieted. Posed with the gavel in midair above the lectern, Runting stared down the loudest group of faculty in the front rows.

"I wish you would have asked these questions and raised these objections a few years ago when our Assessment Committee was preparing our self-study report." Diugud smiled sweetly at the front row. "I would refer you once again to our Higher State assessment plan and invite you to workshops the Teaching and Assessment Center has scheduled this semester."

Without skipping a beat, Diugud summarized what she labeled as the "critical core" of the academic assessment plan.

From what Nicole could gather, the plan concentrated on the classroom level, rejecting mass, standardized testing. It called for "qualitative" rather than quantitative assessment approaches, gathering evidence for improvement rather than accountability, and reporting and discussion primarily at the department level.

"Lord, please make it go away," whispered Ann to Nicole.

"It'll all go away once we give the administration something they can talk up with the accrediting commission and the legislature." Clark gave Nicole what she could only interpret as a polite once-over.

"Our plan integrates assessment into your teaching, course planning, and departmental curriculum development. You embed assessment instruments in your course. By doing so, you'll improve as a teacher and contribute to the overall portrait of educational outcomes at Higher State." Diugud gave the faculty a hands-extended, palms-up "How can we lose?" gesture.

Nicole looked around the room to see how many of the faculty seemed to buy Diugud's appeal. Near the door, Dean Melvin tried to catch Nicole's attention. She quickly averted her gaze. What the heck does he want with me now?

"How do we know if the accrediting commission accepts this approach?" called out a woman near the front. "I don't want to spend time and effort on something that won't satisfy accreditation."

Nicole recognized Selma Skuarrute from the institutional research staff. Felton Bernswaggle once had introduced her as his fiancée. Selma's broad and athletic body seemed destined for grander physiques than poor Bernswaggle's.

"I also wonder how evidence from professors' classrooms without blind scoring and statistical validity tests can pass muster with outside agencies?"

Selma's objections touched off a rambling, esoteric, pro and con debate among many faculty about statistical measurement of academic outcomes. Most of the speakers seemed more interested in simply hearing their own voices and puffing their egos than anything substantive.

Wham!

Runting cracked her gavel down, scaring off further discussion. "We'll take a half-hour break now. Dean Melvin will open our next session and share his thoughts." With that, Runting abruptly exited the lecture hall, the faculty pushing and shoving to follow her out like grade school kids at recess.

"Nicole, let me have a couple of minutes of your time." Dean Melvin steered her down the hall away from the faculty members heading toward the cafeteria. Nicole hoped he wouldn't take long. She needed a sandwich and a cola.

"Ah. Here's Aurelia." Dean Melvin stopped near an alcove with a large window overlooking the campus mall.

"Nicole, as per the continuing investigation and search for Professor

Raskin, we need to know if you have mistakenly opened his closet," said Dean Melvin.

Aurelia and the dean stood in front of Nicole, forcing her to take a step back against the seating bench fitted into the alcove. The pair searched her eyes intently, ready to judge Nicole's answer.

"It was locked. I haven't even been near it," said Nicole.

"Hmmm," went the dean.

"Hmmm," echoed Aurelia.

Were they planning a glee club tryout?

The dean thanked Nicole for her time and urged her to join the faculty for the refreshments in the cafeteria. Aurelia pushed a cell phone at Dean Melvin, a worried look on her face.

CHAPTER 7

Nicole bought a candy bar and a diet soda at a row of stout vending machines, none of which had anything remotely resembling healthful snacks and drinks. Rushing past the cafeteria entrance on the way to her office, she spotted Ann and Maddie surveying a long serving table. The women looked confused by the choices laid out before them. The plates and platters of food Nicole glimpsed didn't look much better than the vending machine fare. Clark MacKenzie dangled a sickly green cluster of grapes at her, smiling in invitation to the feast.

Back in her office, Nicole rushed directly to Raskin's private closet. She tried the steel door. To her surprise, it swung open, revealing a space slightly larger than a telephone booth.

The closet stood empty except for a few dead crawly things on the floor and a spider web swirling from one of the top shelves to the ceiling.

"It's picked clean, lady."

"You scared the hell out of me." Nicole turned to find the city detective who favored bargain-basement ties and shirts.

"What are you looking for in there?"

"Your name and badge number."

"Name's Ron Snife . . . detective with the Normal Police Department." He dug a gold badge out of his back pocket.

Nicole retreated to her side of the office, keeping Raskin's desk between her and the detective. "Have you learned anything new about Professor Raskin?"

"Not a thing breaking so far, but we're hoping the stuff we found in his closet will help."

"But it was locked."

The detective said nothing in return. He stooped to hoist up a large cardboard box. Nicole hadn't noticed it in her rush to check Raskin's closet. She averted her eyes as Detective Snife picked up the box, his low-slung pants separating from his shirt to reveal an appalling décolletage.

Hefting the box, the detective turned back to Nicole, a smile widening across his face. "Don't leave town, I may need to talk with you about the case."

"I bet you say that to all your suspects."

When Nicole arrived at the faculty meeting a few minutes late, Dean Melvin waited at the podium while she made her way past him.

"Last but not least," the Dean trumpeted, "our . . . 'latest' new faculty hire, Nicole Adams."

A few toady faculty laughed for the dean's benefit.

"Now that we're all here, let me address a couple of matters." The dean unbuttoned his suit coat and moved in front of the podium to sit casually on the edge of a table. "Can you still hear me?"

"Of course we can, you dweeb," Nicole muttered under her breath, "your stupid microphone is on."

"We all love Higher State University and look forward to its future greatness. But we stand at a precipice, teetering on the edge of institutional ruin." Dean Melvin paused to let the drama build.

Clark turned around to Nicole. "I saw him this morning practicing with pebbles in his mouth."

"In what? Wing tip sandals?"

Clark looked at Nicole with interest. He had wonderful hazel eyes and long lashes.

"There are forces in the state legislature, within the state university board membership, and yes, individuals lurking in our own community ready to put an end to our educational dreams." Dean Melvin paused again. Despite the inflated rhetoric, he had the faculty's attention.

"We must not give our enemies weapons of destruction to employ against us. We must look deep into our combined consciousness to ferret out weaknesses our critics can turn against us."

"Where does he get this stuff?" asked Maddie.

"It's been a long primary season," said Clark.

Dean Melvin bounced off the table where he had been sitting and advanced to the faculty assembled before him. His eyes looked feverish, but he dialed down his speaking voice a couple of octaves. Nicole guessed he must have entered some sort of Michael Jordan "zone" for college administrators.

"Like an ancient prophet, I deliver a jeremiad—a warning for us to look deep into our academic souls and return to the basic principles of our educational calling."

Several members from the ethnic studies and comparative religion departments raised their hands, frantic to be recognized. Dean Melvin puzzled momentarily at the interruption, but was quick to recognize the political minefield.

"Please, my friends, forgive my incautious rhetorical excess." He paused, building the drama of his pragmatic contrition. "But the problems we face have rocked me to the core."

Like a row of judges, the aggrieved faculty members remained silent but vigilant.

"Rock on, Dean dude," sighed Nicole.

"President Monarck will be here in a minute, but I think I can go ahead and reveal the plan she, the University Council, and our Board of Seers have adopted. The basics of this dynamic response plan were hammered out in the late summer. Unfortunately, the majority of you were absent from campus on vacation."

That last bit of information detonated a spirited protest from one of Nicole's philosophy department colleagues, Rubin Leary, a sixties throwback type. His office's decorative scheme displayed artifacts of his era, including a brilliant Jane Fonda *Barbarella* poster. Rubin had surprised Nicole as she ate lunch one day, pressing her to advise student members of the "Young Militant Vegan Virgins Fast-Food Workers Cadre." Only a sloppy bite of double ChunkieBurger she'd saved from the night before cooled his appeal.

Rubin accused the dean of "off-season" decision making and "oppression of the academic masses." He yelled at the faculty, "When will you pawns quit playing sandbox politics and break up this evil coalition of fat-cat department chairs and sellout management types?"

Before stomping out of the room, Leary delivered a parting shot.

"Pardon me folks, but I've got a meeting with my student customers." His face beet red and his hands shaking, he paused close to Dean Melvin and said something.

Dean Melvin watched the enraged man exit.

"But Rubin, you forgot to call me a 'scum-sucking capitalist pig.'"

Pleased with his taunt, Dean Melvin bounced back to the podium, basking in the faculty's nervous laughter. On his way, he stopped at a chair near the front wall and snatched a stapled packet of angry-looking yellow paper from a huge pile of like objects.

"We call our plan 'Crisis Action Steps: A Commitment to Focus.'" Dean Melvin waved the packet over his head. "Once you've read it, we ask for your immediate approval. We have no time to spare. I counsel you to act in a professional, timely, and responsive manner. Urgency, my friends, urgency is our watchword."

While his office assistants passed out copies of "Crisis Action Steps," Dean Melvin lectured the faculty on governance. He reminded the group that the president had final authority for decision making at Higher State, subject to approval by the Board of Seers. Faculty could only advise and consent, although in Dean Melvin's words, "Without question, the opinions and guidance of the Faculty Association weigh most heavily on our administrative deliberations."

Ann looked bewildered. "The Board of Seers?"

Nicole had no answers. She guessed it was a hangover from the early days of the university.

"A commitment to focus?" Maddie held her eyes wide open. "It sounds scary."

As the dean's minions finished distributing copies of the administration's plan, their boss wrapped up his comments on faculty governance with a warning. "If faculty wish to have a strong hand in decision making, other parties involved in governing our university should expect reasonable dispatch. In addition, faculty must make sure their decisions translate from words to actions and responsibility. If you're going to knit the sweater, you've got to wear it."

These statements muzzled even the most vociferous, critical murmurings among the faculty, though some argued how best to analyze what later would be known as the "dean's sweater."

Nicole doubted anyone had ever raised these touchy issues about faculty governance before. You had to give Buster credit—he didn't pull his punches.

"Dean Melvin, sir, am I hearing you correctly?"

Homer Trout, dressed in his chemistry lab coat, teetering on a gnarled hiking stick, advanced toward the podium. Dean Melvin edged away as Trout tapped his stick on the hardwood floor in anticipation of his next baby step forward.

"Yes, Homer. You heard correctly."

"Let me offer congratulations on your call for responsible and timely action by the faculty. As faculty chair of the president's Select Summer Higher Education Interdisciplinary Team, and as a long-time member of university committees on tenure and promotion, university budget, admissions and financial aid, curriculum reform, core requirements, faculty computer placement, new technology acquisition, fellowships and summer stipends, and . . . oh, yes, athletic ticket distribution"—the deep breath Trout inhaled rattled through his chest—"I applaud your leadership."

Trout reeled off more praise for Dean Melvin, who bowed his head in modesty and humility. With barely a tick of a smile, the dean allowed his ancient acolyte to introduce all other members of the committee who'd helped formulate the Crisis Action plan. Each committee member seemed as fossilized as the diminutive chemist who prattled their names.

One of the chorus girls behind Nicole said, "Every one of them is packing sugar-free fiber pills, Centrum Silver, and twenty-five-year-member AARP cards."

"They're all department chairs, too," added her friend.

"Commitment to focus? Trout'll need a special pill for that," said Maddie.

"Will we need focus groups?" Ann performed a comedian's drum roll.

The "Crisis Action Steps" packet glared at Nicole, small black type contrasting with its yellow background, daring to be read without a magnifying glass. Paging through the double-sided document, she found a six-page introduction followed by three long sections covering the key crisis steps awaiting faculty approval. Nicole pushed the packet into the leather briefcase stowed under her chair. She noticed most of the faculty near her had ignored their packets as well.

Dean Melvin walked over to Trout, who continued to blather at no one in particular. He graced the older man with a protective smile, and gently guided him to a seat. Trout sighed audibly as did his now exhausted, restless listeners.

Refusing to recognize a scattered few faculty indicating a desire to speak, Dean Melvin flicked back his cuff, revealing a shiny gold wristwatch the size of a Yale combination lock.

"It's time now for us to welcome our president, Dr. Thea Monarck." Dean Melvin, pirouetting like Baryshnikov, pointed to the open lecture hall doors to his left.

A small retinue of splendid men and women marched into the room, followed a dramatic three seconds later by President Monarck.

Clad in a pink, nubby wool jacket and matching skirt—set off by jingling gold bracelets stacked on both wrists and a pearl necklace double-looped around a her neck—the president swept by Dean Melvin on her way to the front of the room.

One of her aides plucked the microphone from the dean's neck, buffed it with a handkerchief, and fastened it to the metal holder on the podium. The aide adjusted the microphone to the proper height and stepped back with military precision.

"Thank you so much for attending this gathering, and let me welcome everyone back for this exciting new school year. Higher State

University is indebted to you always for your hard work, talents, and dedication." President Monark jangled a wrist as she carefully patted a section of her hair.

Not much need to worry about your hairdo, thought Nicole. Some perverse hairdresser had shellacked it into a gray batter's helmet.

President Monarck launched into a well-rehearsed recitation of building projects, expansion plans, and fund-raising campaigns for the university.

"I thought we had a financial crisis?" Maddie wrote on the top of the lined pad of paper she'd used for doodling.

"She's an academic Keynesian," Ann scrawled under Maddie's question.

"I know you're busy here with important faculty business, and I have a meeting with the lieutenant governor's staff in Des Moines and a dinner with the Corn County Jaycees." President Monarck smiled at her aides, oblivious to her self-puffery. "I'll wish you all the best for the coming year, and thank you for your support of our 'Crisis Action Steps.'"

With a nod to her staff, the president and the future high-rank academic administrators swept from the room, leaving those who remained feeling somewhat lessened by the absence.

"That's it, then," Corrine Runting told the faculty. "We've been meeting here way past our scheduled adjournment time. Read your 'Crisis Action Steps,' people, and we can talk more about it."

As the faculty in the hall scrapped out of their chairs and gathered up briefcases, notes, purses, and half-finished soft drinks, anxious to leave the hall, Runting yelled for the departmental chairs to stay behind for important business.

Nicole hurried home after grading papers for her morning classes. She'd stayed in her office well into the evening and had her heart set on a frozen spaghetti dinner and slices of French bread. She could pick up the food at the Easy Shoppe on the way. The kitten would probably be waiting for some dinner, too. It showed up each evening for feeding and cuddling, staying part of the night and leaving before Nicole awoke.

Just like my last boyfriend.

Arriving home, she spotted the kitten turning in crazy circles on the porch. In short order, it banged into the flowerpot near the door and flipped over on its back, apparently content to study the petals of Nicole's purple asters.

"What on earth is wrong, kitty?" Nicole lifted the kitten off the porch floor and held up the drooping furry body for a better examination. The animal's eyes wandered and failed to focus, yet it purred like a Ferrari. "You don't look good, you silly fur ball."

Cradling the kitten in one arm, Nicole rushed inside and paged through the university telephone list for the vet school. She reached the emergency number and asked if she could bring the kitten in for a check.

"Hell, yes," answered a bored male voice, "it'll beat the tar out of playing nursemaid to a three-hundred-pound hog with gastritis."

Nicole placed the kitten in a cardboard book box and raced out to her car.

CHAPTER 8

"You had one stoned kitty cat, Professor."

"But how could that happen?" As promised, the vet student had called Nicole at her office that morning.

"Well, I doubt the poor thing rolled its own stuff. It must have grazed on some first-rate grass in your neighborhood."

"How can you tell it was marijuana?" asked Nicole.

"I do drug testing all the time for the athletic department. It's a way to earn a few extra bucks. I borrowed one of the test kits and did a blood sample. Your kitty won't be playing outside linebacker once I file the NCAA drug test report."

Nicole thanked the aspiring veterinarian for his help and arranged to pick up the kitten after classes that day. She promised herself to look for suspicious weeds around the neighborhood.

Once the faculty had an opportunity to read "Crisis Action Steps: A Commitment to Focus," an immediate and agitated reaction swept through the ranks. Most professors now referred to the plan post-colon—with appropriate alterations—and according to a newly emerged post-colon, postmodernist faculty clique, the altered wording clearly represented a "deprivatization of a signified passion."

No one seemed more affected by a close reading of the plan packet than the steadfast sixties radical, Rubin Leary.

"Have you read what the ruling-class pond scum are planning?"

Rubin had intercepted Nicole outside her classroom. He wore his thinning gray hair in a ponytail, secured with what looked like a string of red plastic ties from bread packages. His black T-shirt, featuring a fading Jimi Hendrix image, had seen better days, but his satin, blue, shin-length, hip-hop basketball shorts sported a recent price tag at the waist. The argyle socks and sandals Rubin wore somehow made his outfit perversely complete.

"Have you read page six?" Rubin didn't wait for an answer. "They're going to revise the admissions standards and the core curriculum, dude. It blows my mind."

"How's that supposed to solve our problems?" Nicole asked.

"The dean and his dimwits are calling it a 'Transactional Matrix.' They say it'll open up equality of access and opportunity for disadvantaged students to realize the American Dream. Truth is, it's a scheme to increase the student pool so the damn place won't go broke. It'll be a disaster for the good students we have."

Rubin hauled a plastic baggie out of the large laundry sack he used for a briefcase and offered Nicole what looked like granola. "Try it, girl. It's my own blend."

The pair sat on a bench in the spacious atrium entrance of the Robert Hall classroom complex. Students paraded past a large fountain and water-lily pool encircled by a low wall covered with multihued glazed tiles. Fountain spray surged outward at various heights each minute from the base of massive statuary. Demeter, the Greek goddess of grain and fertility, awaiting the return of her daughter, Persephone, rose upward almost two stories to a cloud-shaped skylight. Hermes, messenger of the gods, standing to the side, rated only a small part within the fountain tableau. But Hermes drew the attention of those passing by. His groin had been draped with what looked like a rubber kilt styled to look like laurel leaves.

"I love this building," Rubin said, munching a carefully selected handful of nuts. Nicole noticed he alternated nuts with raisins and wondered if he sequenced the health food for an optimum benefit.

"Old Lazlo O'Callaghan designed the whole thing, including all the art work." Rubin jammed home another handful of nuts. "I miss hanging with that crazy dude."

Nicole made a note to learn more about O'Callaghan. His name also graced a brass cornerstone plate at DeTassell Hall.

Switching subject gears, Rubin said, "In principle, I like democratizing higher education. Participatory democracy begs for a widely educated citizenry. But it's scary to have every Dick and Jane marching into the hallowed halls of ivy."

Nicole resolved to read the fine print on the Crisis Action plan. She knew admission to Higher State University required a 2.5 high school grade average and a minimum 18 out of 36 on the ACT exams.

"During my sabbatical year I buzzed out of this cow town and back to San Francisco. I couldn't afford it, so I taught a bunch of classes at a local college." Rubin picked at the threads holding the price tag on his shorts. "Much as I'd like to mess with the faculty snots here, I wouldn't wish unprepared masses of students on anybody. We already have our share."

Rubin munched some more and lapsed into a troubled silence.

Nicole thought about her cousin Ruth. She had enough intelligence to be a great college student. She'd always read interesting books and could more than hold her ground during holiday gatherings when the family argued everything from foreign policy to music. Ruth quit high school in her senior year and tried to make a go of it as an artist. Three years later, homeless and without a high school diploma, Ruth returned to Minneapolis with the promise she would enroll at the community college after passing her GED. Nicole would love to have students with Ruth's potential in her classes.

"I liked an awful lot of the students out in San Francisco, and I worked my butt off trying to teach all of them," Rubin picked up strands of his community college story again, "but you ended up with such a wide disparity between the students in the classes. I couldn't figure out who to teach."

"What do you mean?"

"It boiled down to three groups. The class limit was thirty-five students. In every class, I had about five students who could have gone to a four-year university or a good private college . . . if they could have afforded it. Hell, some of them didn't know about applying for scholarships. About ten had some promise and improved as the semester went along. They got used to my teaching and going to school." Rubin watched a group of students gathered by the fountain near the figure of Hermes, laughing at the rubber kilt.

"The rest of the students had no business being in a college classroom. It wasn't that they were bad kids—they simply weren't ready to do the work. Most of them couldn't read or write at a college level, and I had some foreign students who couldn't understand English well enough to take notes or participate in discussion. It really burned me to see those folks exploited by the school."

"How were they exploited? They had the chance to go to college." Nicole noticed Clark MacKenzie walk down the curving steps into the atrium. She waved him over.

Rubin looked at Nicole like she had failed recess.

"They were exploited because the college took their tuition money, sold them overpriced textbooks, and sent them into classes where they'd be sure to fail. No testing and no required remediation to help students know what they could reasonably handle in college-level courses. On top of that, there were too few remedial classes and too many students needing help. Talk about shoddy ethics." Rubin rolled his eyes.

Clark sat on the bench next to Nicole. He squeezed her arm in greeting. "Are you trying to recruit this innocent to some revolutionary cell, Rubin?"

"No, man, we were rapping about the dean's counterrevolution." Rubin shifted his attention back to Nicole, a sad frown creased his face. "Out in San Francisco, some of the really good students and the ones with promise probably didn't learn close to what they should have in my class. They were stuck in there with too many classmates who couldn't do the work or didn't want to."

"Maybe you should have taught to their level and forgot about the ones who couldn't hack the work," said Clark. "You can't teach everybody that shows up."

"That sounds really crusty, Clark." Nicole didn't like to admit it, but she faced the same issues in her introductory classes at Higher State. She hated the idea of writing off so many students and often wondered if professors at the better colleges and universities had to face anywhere near the same problems. They ought to spend a few days in the minor leagues and count their blessings.

"I don't mean to sound so harsh, but what's the alternative?" Clark looked to Rubin and Nicole for an answer. "We have the same issue here, don't we?"

Bent forward, elbows on knees, Rubin kneaded his temples. A small tattoo of Chairman Mao peeked out from under the sleeve of his T-shirt. "You are so right, man. The math department did a statistical breakdown of final grades in their gen-ed courses. Basically, they had A students, and C and below students—without much in between."

"And the majority were C and below, right? We did the same thing in our department," said Clark.

Nicole often felt like the good students in her class were the victims. The majority in her introductory classes seemed to make it difficult for the most talented and motivated students to learn.

"It really makes things hard when half of my students don't keep up with the reading," said Nicole. "I have a feeling some of them have never even bought the books, and the others—"

"It's soooo hard and it's soooo 'like boring.'"

Clark's imitation carried farther than he intended, and some of the students sitting nearby on the fountain border glared at him.

"They bitch about the textbook, and mine's a good one—very readable and has lots of good supplementary stuff," said Clark. "I asked them today if they'd bought the historical novel that's due in two weeks. About half the class just plain admitted they hadn't. I couldn't believe it."

"They won't have to read one-eighth of the pages I did for most of my undergraduate courses," said Nicole. "I'm about to make the articles in the readings book I assigned into extra credit."

Rubin leaned back, laughing. "They'll love that. By the end of the semester you'll be ready to shoot the next student who asks if he can do something for extra credit."

"I'm amazed at how many of my students keep asking questions about things I have clearly spelled out in the syllabus." Nicole recalled an exchange with her students the hour before for Rubin and Clark. She'd warned her logic class about the upcoming exam and had set a date for a review session.

"Let me guess." Clark gave Rubin a knowing look, and slipped into his student imitation, "Will it be multiple choice?"

Rubin didn't miss a beat. "Can we use our notes?"

"If we miss the test for work or something, when's the makeup?" Clark countered.

Nicole thought about adding her favorite, "I lost my study guide for the textbook" (despite the fact she hadn't written a study guide).

"Oh boy, here comes trouble." Rubin edged backward on the bench, trying to hide behind Nicole. "It's Hildie Knochblauster . . . swami of the college teaching center . . . virtuoso of the teaching circle . . . queen bee of faculty development . . ."

Hildie, laden with two canvas bags from the campus bookstore, a cavernous leather purse, and a batch of brightly colored handouts stashed under her arm, lurched toward their bench.

"Have you decided yet about the teaching workshop next week, Rubin?" Hildie allowed the two book bags and black purse to drop at her feet with a thud and rush of dust from the floor. Her upper lip gleamed with tiny beads of sweat.

When Rubin mumbled something, Hildie converted the mumble to a positive answer. "Good. We'll see you there. Our session is titled 'Students Controlling Their Own Learning.'"

"Don't they do that now?" Rubin rubbed his forehead.

Hildie gave Rubin an affectionate tap on his shoulder. "It's the wave of the future, Mr. Old School. You can't keep moaning and groaning about how things used to be."

"I tried some of your ideas in my class last semester, and the student evaluations said they hated group work and stuff like that. I felt like some damn est therapist," Rubin frowned, looking glum, "and none of my students 'got it.'"

Nicole felt sorry for Hildie. "I'll pull over another bench. Go ahead and sit."

Hildie sat between the two men like a girl at a dance party for ten-year-olds.

Rubin tried to ignore her, tossing the baggie with the crumbled remains of his snack into a trash receptacle. "I hope we don't start teaching like some the professors I've heard about. To keep up enrollments, they really lowered their standards. Simple quizzes, 'multiple guess' exams, no research papers, and the students hardly had to read anything but a textbook."

"I don't think we have to sacrifice standards." Hildie brushed some granola crumbs from Rubin's pant leg, her brightly painted nails snagging the satin material. "But we need to better understand our students, don't you think? We have to adapt to changes in our student body and find new ways to teach without losing what we treasure about higher education and our teaching careers."

Nicole wanted to agree with Hildie, but her mind filled with images of her students. At that moment, except for that small minority in each class, she'd rather forget they existed than beat her head against a wall trying to understand them. It didn't seem right to feel that way. Maybe every new teacher went through the same feelings.

"I've got a class in ten minutes," Rubin said, checking the contents of his laundry sack cum briefcase. "Got a quick fix for me, Hildie?"

The eyes behind the stylish blue-rimmed glasses softened and Hildie laughed at the rumpled man standing before her. She leaned over and snatched at her bags, the effort of bending over coloring her cheeks. Clark handed her the purse she couldn't reach and helped her rise from the low bench. Nicole pictured the woman twenty years younger. She would have been quite attractive—her naturally curly hair and beautiful skin undiminished by the years.

Hildie whispered something to Rubin and brushed past him. He watched her walk away, his mouth dropped open and eyes wide. He shook his head, but remained without comment for Nicole and Clark's benefit.

"Are you taking off?" Nicole asked Rubin.

"I have another class."

"Before you go, tell me what's with Hermes' kilt?"

"A long story, Nicole. Let's just say Lazlo's original design erected the Hermes statue in a manner some found offensive."

As he reached the steps leading down past the fountain to the building's entrance, Rubin paused. "Hey, this was fun. Let's make it a regular occasion."

Nicole and Clark nodded their agreement and watched Rubin join a flock of students heading out of the building.

The kitten scratched at the screen door and mewed softly. She'd lounged on the sagging armchair ever since Nicole had brought her back from the vet school. But a warm canopy of stars in a purple early evening sky and the sounds of slithering, crawling things outside proved more inviting to the kitten than more time at rest.

"Let's go for a walk, Munchkin." Nicole thought it fitting to christen her feline companion, as it seemed certain now the kitten would be a permanent guest resident.

Munchkin bounced across the lawn, happy to be outside. She made a beeline to the wall that separated the house property from the DeTassell Institute. Nicole followed the kitten as it dashed behind the overgrown red sumac bush.

Nicole ducked under the sumac and stepped forward, one hand feeling for the opening in the brick wall. She fished around in the side pocket of her cargo pants for her key chain with the miniflashlight. Within the thin beam of light, Munchkin sat before the wall, scratching with one paw against new bricks covering the former opening.

CHAPTER 9

TENDE ALTIUS

The clock radio next to Nicole's bed blasted her from a deep sleep at 6:00 a.m. The student announcer on WHSU's morning program, *Normal Music and News for Misfits*, chattered about upcoming exams and the mid-October homecoming weekend. "Thanks to Chris Columbus, it'll be a three-day bash. So party on, scholars, and hang with us for the ride. Here's one going out for Nina, Pinta, and Santa Maria."

Nicole couldn't wait for the long weekend. The first part of the semester had flown past. She needed a break from preparing classes, the demands of faculty activities, and Dean Melvin's special assignments.

Before classes started that morning, Nicole planned to finish drafting her course exams. At lunchtime she would meet Clark in the library. He'd proposed they search the archives for information about Lazlo O'Callaghan.

Clark had dropped by Nicole's office the day before and puzzled over Raskin's closet. He'd found the missing philosophy professor's long shelf of books on art and architecture equally perplexing.

"I love a mystery," he'd said. "Want to do some historical sleuthing?"

Nicole figured this might be Clark's way of asking for a date, and she'd accepted his invitation to visit the archives. Maybe she'd invite Clark out for dinner tonight if their venture into the past proved a success. She remembered a quote from a list her undergraduate history professor had given students: "No historian should be trusted implicitly."

She could always hope.

Nicole found her faculty mailbox overflowing with publisher's book advertisements, university newsletters, and a glut of meeting announcements. These calls to duty arrived on stiff paper stock of various hues emblazoned with blaring fonts. The announcements urged faculty to meet and discuss the new admissions criteria and the proposal to revise the core curriculum. It seemed to Nicole that the decisions had already been made. Would faculty debate at this point make any sense?

"Dean Melvin's timing is impeccable, is it not?"

Horace Phillips, visiting African American sociologist from Georgetown, smiled at Nicole as he separated meeting announcements from a considerable number of important-looking envelopes. He dropped the announcements into the recycling barrel as if they were rotting fish.

Nicole stole a glance at the first-class mail he had placed on the narrow shelf in front of the mailboxes. She could see the raised logos and addresses of several prestigious universities. The one item of first-class mail Nicole had received in the past weeks had been an unpaid fee notice from the University of Minnesota.

"Seems like Dean Melvin, supreme commander of the good ship Higher State, has launched his reform initiative at a time when faculty are terribly busy giving exams and grading." Horace had a deep and sonorous voice, and with his commanding physical stature, he filled the small room with his presence.

It was true. Nicole had found little time since the faculty meeting to do anything, much less fully read the Crisis Action plan. The small print and deadly prose of the document consigned it to a far corner of her desk.

Horace leaned back against the mailbox shelf, a playful look in his eyes. "I'm particularly taken with the proposed master's track in Evangelical Organizational Management. Praise the Lord and pass the MBAs."

"Hi, Nicole." Rubin Leary popped into the claustrophobic space of the mailroom.

"What's happening, Horace?"

Horace nodded a pleasant greeting. "Damn, Rubin, where did you find those threads?"

Rubin wore a colorful Mexican serape over a kaleidoscopic, tie-dyed T-shirt—the colors of the respective garments locked in combat. His seventies-style corduroy bell-bottom pants, a tasteful ruby maroon color, draped to the floor, allowing but a peek at bright red Chuck Taylor Converse All-Star basketball shoes.

"Those look like the same tennies you had when we played ball in high school," said Horace.

"You two know each other from high school?" Nicole looked in surprise from one man to the other.

Rubin stepped next to Horace, the top of his head barely reaching the other man's shoulder. "Yeah. This big dude and I grew up together right here in Normal. Known each other for way too long."

"My mom still lives here in town, and Rubin landed me a one-semester gig so I could have a long visit," said Horace.

While the two men recalled highlights of their senior basketball season, Clark wandered in and stood next to Nicole.

Finished recounting a stirring overtime victory in a long-past basketball tournament, Rubin waved the familiar yellow "Crisis Action Steps" packet at the group. He turned back several wrinkled pages, his index finger searching the rows of print, and motioned Nicole to take a look.

"Scope this out—our newly proposed 'Credits for Experiential Learning.' Tell me it's not all about counting bodies and courting the capitalists."

Nicole smoothed out the document. In a few sentences, it introduced a plan to allow students to receive college credits—equated to courses in the Higher State University curriculum—for knowledge achieved through a variety of work and learning experiences.

"Is there no end to the possibilities for acquiring college credit at our esteemed institution?" Bob Olufssen entered the mailroom and whispered a brief hello in Nicole's ear. Clark gave him a cool appraisal, which to Nicole's point of view seemed . . . pleasantly territorial.

"Bobby-boy, I'd have thought you would be on the bandwagon 100 percent for this one," said Rubin.

"Rubin. Must you always be such a nasty . . . dude?"

Nicole concluded the two were not amigos.

Bob asked if he could borrow the Crisis Action plan packet and scanned a couple of paragraphs. "I can't buy this. Not only does it promise credits for passing standardized national tests, CLEP and that sort, but . . . it goes further to say, and I quote, 'students can initiate other evaluation mechanisms the university may develop and approve.'"

Bob flicked his finger against the page with a loud snap. "What the hell does that mean? It's a license to steal college credits. Besides, I want students to learn foreign language through my methods and from my teaching faculty."

"My, my," Horace shifted his bulk off the shelf to tower over Bob.

"But if a student knows a subject, why should she have to waste time in a class repeating it?" asked Clark.

Nicole liked Clark's choice of pronouns. She also thought he had a good point.

What difference did it make where you learned something? Her Uncle Ethan had been a supervisor at an industrial plant for twenty years. If he ever went to college, did he have to sit through Management 101? Did he have to be taught by some professor who had little or no real business experience? As to Bob's objection, Nicole had learned more French during the year she spent as an exchange student in Paris than in any classroom.

Bob touched his hand to Nicole's shoulder, as if assuming she'd be on his side of the discussion. "So Clark, can you imagine giving a student college credit in history, equivalent to some course you teach, for reading *she* might have done about World War II or something like that?"

"Why not?" Nicole shrugged off Bob's proprietary hand. "You

don't need someone to teach you each and every subject in a classroom."

"I agree." Clark said to Bob, the two confronting each other within the small space remaining in the mailroom. Nicole's mind flashed on dueling elks in the Pacific Northwest.

"If I couldn't have received credit for my prior life and career learning, I wouldn't be standing here now." Sonja Helgerson, an assistant professor in the math department stood barely inside the door, searching for a way to her mailbox. She looked back over her shoulder, "If anyone else shows up here, the students will think it's an orgy."

Horace backed out of the way so Sonja could slip past him and retrieve her mail. Everyone else in the crowded space shifted in one way or another to accommodate another body. Bob used the occasion to press close to Nicole.

She'd not noticed his smarmy cologne before.

"I know your story, Sonja," said Horace, "but maybe Professor Olufssen needs to hear it." He reached out and guided Bob closer to Sonja, winking at Nicole as he did.

"Well, the *Reader's Digest* version is simple. When my husband died, I had a young child, about a year of college, and a small amount of life insurance. I needed a college degree to earn a decent living. In the five years Arnie and I were married, his company had us in Japan for two years before we moved back to New York City. Until Libby came along, I had lots of free time. I was in a great book discussion group and I did some counseling at a juvenile detention center. I enrolled in continuing education classes at museums and community arts centers, and before we went to Japan, I studied Japanese at Berlitz."

Sonja hesitated before continuing her story, perhaps to judge if any listeners might object. Bob turned to his mailbox slot.

"So tell them where you started your climb to stardom in academe." Horace folded his arms across his chest and gave the older woman an encouraging smile.

"I don't want to hold up anyone with my dramatic tale."

"I have to get ready for my class." Bob worked his way to the door.

It would have been polite to wait a few minutes, Nicole thought.

She tried to cover Bob's unapologetic exit by asking Sonja to finish her story.

"OK. I was living in Minneapolis with my mother when a new state university opened for adult, nontraditional students like myself. The advisors encouraged me to develop what I had learned into a form that could be evaluated and awarded college credits."

Sonja described a complex process she had completed to receive college credit for what she called her "prior learning" experiences. First she took a noncredit workshop on how to identify college-level learning from life and work experience. Then she had to write a formal proposal for each subject she wanted to have evaluated and find an approved university evaluator.

"After a few other bureaucratic, but reasonable, steps I had my evaluation of learning." Sonja waved her hands in front of her like a magician. "I had a good number of credits that counted for general education and graduation electives. Eventually, I saved a lot of time and earned my BA degree in two and a half years."

"What were some of the credits you earned?" Clark sounded a bit confused by the explanation. Nicole wasn't quite sure herself how an evaluation would work.

"Let's see. I earned six semester credits in Japanese and three each in Japanese art history, printmaking, classics of American literature, and public speaking." Sonja stuffed her mail into battered briefcase. "Oh, and I completed a theory seminar on counseling and one on volunteerism."

"Theory seminar?"

"My university developed what it called theory seminars. To earn prior learning credits, you need a healthy understanding of theory in a subject. It can't only be practical experience. I'd done about two years' worth of counseling in New York and some in Minneapolis at a youth shelter. But I didn't have much knowledge about, say, current counseling theories or some of the legal and ethical issues. Three sessions of the seminar, along with assigned independent reading and research, prepared me for my evaluation."

Nicole asked if Sonja could answer one last question. "How do you determine if something like your 'Classics of American Literature' is college level?"

"Easy." Sonja paused at the doorway leading to the hall, "The university had a two-semester course I could use for comparison. If they hadn't, I could have demonstrated that a reputable college or university taught a similar course. But I still had to pass my evaluation before I received any credit."

"So how did you end up as a mathematician?" asked Rubin.

"Somebody's got to do it." Sonja waved and breezed into a crowd of students heading toward their next hour's classes.

Clark peeled a banana he'd dug out from his book bag. "What do you think, Rubin? Is the dean on to something here?

Rubin curled his lip and gave a soft growl. "If so, it's for the worst of reasons. It's all about enrollments and money."

"But why wouldn't it be good policy if done right?" Horace edged around a partition to the coffee urn, his head and shoulders still visible because of his height. "Come on, Rubin, whatever happened to that educational radical I used to know?"

"Horace, our power structure isn't proposing all these reforms on principle, and besides, the faculty wouldn't want to put in all the work."

Rubin looked around at those remaining in the room. No one cared to challenge his point.

Nicole and Clark met at the library archives and spent well over an hour searching through past campus newspapers, photos, yearbooks, and other collected materials on the university's early history. They also located a listing of a couple of brief oral histories taped by students in a history course in 1981. Professors Raskin and Leary, along with Dean Melvin and Aurelia Castle were on the list. The new librarian, Polly Cimale, promised she'd locate the box of tapes.

"We have a load of stuff I haven't cataloged, gathering dust in the storage room," she said.

"We've got to get back here soon and listen to those interviews," said Clark, guiding Nicole out the front doors of the library. The couple blinked against the glare of the midday sunshine.

"I'd like to know more about the connections between all these folks." Nicole rubbed her eyes and tried to look up at Clark.

"I could write a monograph from what we've found about Lazlo."

"I think you had better concentrate on the publications you promised in your last tenure review with the Dean," a voice from behind warned Clark.

Aurelia Castle's all-black outfit made her nearly invisible standing in the shade of a large pillar—one of many gracing the entrance to the library. Aurelia emerged from the shadow into the light and nodded at Nicole. "Don't forget, my gallant young historian, you are up for tenure this year."

The dean's assistant moved close to Clark and used a red fingernail to illustrate as she whispered, "It'll be *up* or *down* this time."

CHAPTER 10

Several students in the ethics class grimaced and shifted uneasily at their desks. Some stole glances at Nicole, their eyes accusatory and fearful. Others stared off into space, the paper in front of them as blank as their faces. A few wretched souls gazed with envy at Nicole's best students, scratching away with their pens, rapidly filling the spaces on their exam sheets.

As she looked at the classroom scene unfolding before her, Nicole wanted to tell her students, "It shouldn't be that hard, people."

She had constructed a variety of simple situations involving ethical reasoning and choices, always based on what her class had read and discussed. Her syllabus explained what to expect on exams, and she'd given some general advice in class about taking this first exam.

Only one student had asked a question. "You mean there won't be any multiple choice?" Nicole briefly considered initiating a discussion about ethics and multiple choices, but answered the student's question with a simple "No."

At the beginning of the hour, Nicole had asked her students to hand in the three-page response paper assigned at the start of the semester and due that day. She thought the assignment would motivate most students as it allowed them to write about situations they might face in their college years. Nicole noticed that five students did not pass forward their papers as requested.

While she monitored the exam, Nicole recalled what she and Clark had discovered on their library excursion. The most surprising revelation had come in a box of photographs. Judging by the hairstyles and clothing, these pictures dated from the seventies.

"Look at this unbelievable group portrait I found." Nicole passed a large print across the table.

In the photo, several men and women posed on the steps of DeTassell Hall. The caption at the bottom of the photo read, "HSU's Founding Leaders and Faculty Gather for the Dedication at DeTassell Hall." A typewritten sheet affixed to the back named the faculty in the photo, and a short paragraph described the 1978 ceremony and identified the building's architect as Lazlo O'Callaghan.

Nicole and Clark studied the print, flipping it over to match each figure with the names listed on the back.

"Look at these folks." Clark traced around a group lounging on the wide set of marble steps leading into the building.

Nicole could identify a younger, smiling Professor Raskin. He stood with his arm linked to a handsome man with a full black beard, dressed up like someone straight out of the Renaissance. It was Lazlo O'Callaghan, according to the listing.

Clark turned the photo toward him and squinted at one of the figures.

"Who's the woman next to Raskin? Sorry, but she is really something."

"Well, stop salivating on the picture and look her up on the list."

Clark concentrated on the task, flipping the print over a couple of times. A slow smile spread across his face. "Guess who?"

"Clark. Cut the crap."

"Are you ready for this? It's Ingrid . . . Raskin."

Polly returned from the storage room with a metal box labeled "1991—interview tapes." Judging by the dust-covered box and the strands of ancient spider webs affixed to the back of Polly's sweater, no one had touched the container for years. Polly promised she would keep it safe until Nicole and Clark returned the next day.

"Do I assume we want to keep all this as quiet as possible?"

"We'd prefer it that way," Clark said.

Polly put a finger to her lips and placed the small metal box behind a pile of government documents in a far corner of the room. She seemed to relish the intrigue—so much so she returned to the table and hung over Clark's shoulder as he continued examining the photo. Polly squeezed past Nicole and from a chain dangling on her neck applied a small magnifier to the photo's surface.

"It's the archivist's best friend," she said, enlarging the beautiful face of Ingrid Raskin. "Oh my. Wasn't she a beauty?"

"You mean Raskin's wife?" asked Nicole.

"No. That's Mrs. James DeTassell. I met her at the 'Friends of the Library' fund-raiser last week."

"Professor Adams." The abrasive voice from the front-row desk surprised Nicole, and the book she'd been holding fell to the floor with a loud "thwaack."

"Sorry. Keep working," she told the class.

Nicole picked up the book and made her way to speak with the young woman who had interrupted her thoughts. "What's the problem, Ashley?"

"I really studied hard for this exam, and I don't know these."

Ashley pointed a finger at some of the ethical concepts and philosophers Nicole had listed on the exam. She'd supplied the list as an aid for her students' written responses as they examined a series of ethics cases. The students had argued for a list of that sort, and Nicole didn't see any reason not to provide one. The names and concepts baffling Ashley had been drawn from the readings book, but Nicole had not discussed all the articles in class.

"Why can't we use our notes? I can't memorize every single one of these names and all the other stuff." Amber Schultz, her eyes alight with good-natured mischief, sat next to Ashley.

A likable student, Amber knew how to push the right buttons—all the while exuding a teenage charm. In the previous class session, Nicole had mentioned how much she had hated to memorize names and dates for exams. It appeared Amber had filed that information away for the right moment.

Nicole glanced at the room clock. The hour had only twenty minutes remaining. "OK. Fine. Use your notes if you want."

Her students bent and snatched at backpacks stored at their feet, rifling through their books and papers.

"Can we use our books?" Ashley pleaded.

Nicole shook her head and smiled. "Please don't ask why."

During the remaining minutes of the exam, the students shuffled through notebooks and note cards, every once in a while stopping to scribble answers. Nicole saw too many students shuffling instead of scribbling, although she could have predicted their misdirected efforts. She also rightly figured that several of the hat-backward boys and other scholastic miscreants would come up empty-handed. They never took notes in her class—almost as if they didn't know they should.

Nicole took advantage of the student's preoccupation with the exam to "Google" Lazlo O'Callaghan on the computer sunken into the teaching platform. The university archives had yielded very little useful information about him. Her preliminary Internet search revealed an artist of considerable talents whose relative obscurity had ended in the late 1990s. Following Lazlo's unexpected death in 2002, relatives in San Francisco had discovered three paintings among his household effects, dating from the late 1970s. As the article in the e-zine reported, "a jury of experts on twentieth-century American folk art valued the three small paintings by Lazlo O'Callaghan at well over two million dollars. The recently deceased artist's work has won favor with critics in the last few years. O'Callaghan's paintings and sculptures from his 'green Melmac' period, dating to his last years in San Francisco 1993–2002, have skyrocketed. Very few early paintings or sculptures from his formative years at a small university in Iowa are extant. As critic Saz Morimoto estimates, 'Anyone in possession of O'Callaghan's early artwork is in for a pleasant financial surprise.'"

Nicole recalled the article about O'Callaghan in the Normal *News Register* near the start of the semester. She found the online archives for the newspaper and searched for O'Callaghan. She read through the article she remembered from late August, "Former HSU Artist's Work Earns Hefty Payoff." Taken from a report in the Associated Press, the article revealed that a relatively unknown San Francisco art dealer had auctioned off an O'Callaghan painting from 1979 for over $600,000. Jade Knowles, the art dealer and owner of the Berkeley Art Cooperative and Organic Foods, had told an interviewer, "the sky's the limit for these early O'Callaghans."

At the close of the hour, two distinct types of students advanced toward Nicole. One group with only a few sentences scrawled on their papers slouched to the front. They buried their exams in the growing pile or turned up the backside so Nicole couldn't read their names. Most of their handwriting was sloppy and difficult to read. The other group smiled at Nicole and deposited their exams neatly in front of her. Not only had these students written more in the answer sections, but their handwriting could be easily deciphered. To Nicole's surprise, Dan Wilson, who sat in the very back row and never said a thing in discussion, handed her an exam that looked very promising.

"I could have written a lot more," said Dan. Nicole reminded herself to draw the young man out in future class discussions. Those discussions had taken a positive turn lately as Nicole had crammed in some quick research at the library on college teaching strategies. A small step, perhaps, but the classroom activities buoyed her spirits. She hoped the students would surprise her on the exam, despite what she had seen.

A few stragglers continued to work on their exams after the bell rang. Ricky O'Keefe, a major-league shortstop prospect with minor-league study habits, passed Nicole his exam. He remained standing next to her, his lips set in a thin line. "I didn't hand in my response paper, Professor."

"Why is that, Ricky? You knew it was due today."

Ricky shifted back and forth, stubbing the toe of his running shoe against the floor. "Grandmother died this weekend."

Nicole hated dealing with students' excuses, but predicted she'd hear a carload from those who'd failed to hand in their papers or missed the exam. Her voice mail already had four messages from students, each claiming transmission failure. Did she have to become a car mechanic as well as a philosopher to teach?

"Can I hand it in next week?" Ricky asked. "I got slowed down because we started our fall baseball series with Drake this week."

Nicole recalled something an older graduate student friend had warned her about when they assisted in Dr. Osgood's course. "Listen carefully to the excuses and analyze what the students say."

"You said 'Grandmother' passed away, Ricky. Is that correct?"

Ricky averted his eyes, studying the baseball cap he held in his hand. "Was it *your* grandmother?"

Ricky couldn't master the moment, and he struggled to suppress the grin inching upward from the corners of his mouth. He plopped his baseball cap back over laughing eyes. "So can I get it to you tomorrow?"

"Yes. But you'll receive a grade one level below what you might earn." Nicole left Ricky where he stood.

Outside her office door, five students waited, each with well-practiced "woe-is-me" looks plastered on their faces. Nicole made an abrupt about-face and headed to the basement of her building, searching for Hildie Knochblauster's office in the Center for Teaching Excellence.

Hildie removed a pair of reading glasses from the tip of her nose, appraising Nicole as she collapsed into an aging, but comfortable, sofa.

"Let me get you a cup of green tea." Hildie poured Nicole a steaming cup of fragrant liquid from an elegant Japanese tea set. The teaching center's director settled back into her leather desk chair and sipped from her teacup, her gaze fixed on Nicole.

In a soothing voice, flavored with a comic German accent, Hildie asked, "Vood you like to talk about it?"

"Ja, Doktor Hildie, I vood," Nicole kicked off her shoes and lay back on the sofa.

After Nicole completed the account of her exam experience, Hildie sighed and pulled out a drawer from a huge complex of file cabinets. She flicked through several folders in the drawer before selecting a file.

"Here's our 'Excuuuse Me! Teaching Tips Handouts for Frustrated Faculty.'" It should give you ideas about how to handle those pesky moments of creative storytelling." Hildie slid a classy looking trifold brochure across her desk. "More important, it'll also tell you how to stop the excuses before they start."

Nicole noticed the handout's first section bore the subtitle, "But I Gave It to Your Secretary . . ."

"You realize this is but the tip of the iceberg, don't you?"

Nicole pulled one of the sofa's pillows over her face. "You mean grading their exams and papers?"

Hildie poured more tea into her cup, tilting the teapot at Nicole to see if she wanted a refill. "You'll want to be prepared for the next phase of agitation. The worst part can be explaining to students why they received a certain grade, especially when you have them writing essays and papers. We seem to have a lot of students here who get very upset and pushy when it comes to grading."

Nicole groaned and scrunched farther down into the sofa. Grading all the exams and papers would be punishment enough. Handling a raft of student complaints and arguing about grades would be hell. As a grad assistant, she could always claim to disgruntled students that she had no control over what the professor asked them to do and how they were graded.

"Here are some questions new instructors should ask themselves about grading." Hildie tossed another trifold pamphlet that landed on Nicole's stomach. "There are a lot of ways to go about grading, and they often depend on the subject. But we can identify what is effective grading."

Nicole didn't want to admit it, but she had little idea of what effective grading would be for her courses. She sat up and pulled her shoes back on, stealing a glance at the grading pamphlet lying next to her. One of the subtitles caught her attention, "Save Time! Start Planning Your Grading from Day One." She groaned, rolling off the sofa and retrieving her purse as she stood.

"Thanks Hildie. I'm sure these will be a real help."

"You may want to sign up for the effective grading workshop in January."

Hildie tapped the eraser of her pencil on her lower lip, a knowing but sympathetic expression crossing her face as Nicole backed toward the door.

Following her afternoon classes and a quick bite at the student union, Nicole resolved to start grading. As it grew dark outside her office window, she cleared the surface of her desk and withdrew two red-ink ballpoint pens from her drawer. She placed the stack of ethics response papers front and center, along with her grade book.

She spent a few minutes daydreaming about a vacation in Mexico and tuning the small AM-FM radio to a classical music station before pulling the first paper off the stack.

After marking several spelling and grammatical errors with bold slashes of red ink, she flipped the offending document to the side. She searched the stack for a paper from a good student. While no errors glared from the first page of Brianna Brooks' essay, she hadn't built a reasoned argument using the reading sources and lectures.

Nicole dug again through the pile, searching for a paper that might capture what she had intended for the assignment. Some students came close. Most didn't for a variety of reasons—too much personal opinion, unsubstantiated arguments, poor organization, digressions, and misunderstandings about the readings.

The ballpoint pen clattered to the floor as Nicole gave in to despair. She felt that grading these papers would take forever, especially if she made all the promised corrections and suggestions. She still faced grading the exams from this class and the two sections of logic. Nicole spread her arms around the papers before her and lowered her forehead into their midst.

She dreamed of home . . . of her family's house in southwest Minneapolis . . . of her room. In her dream, she studied for her most difficult high school subject ever—chemistry. As she willed herself to memorize the confusing symbols and formulas, loud clunks and scraping noises sounded in the garage next to her room. She turned to the strange man sitting on her bed, who quizzed her on the periodic tables. *What's the use? I'll never pass the test.* She needed some sympathy, a pat on the back. The man on the bed sneered at her and enjoyed her discomfort.

"Hey. Wake up." The hand on her shoulder made Nicole jump.

"Oh, Clark." Nicole felt dizzy and took a deep, gulping breath. "I was having a horrible dream."

"I thought we were going to listen to those tapes."

Nicole tried to rub away the sleep wrinkles she knew crinkled her check. Peeping out at Clark between her fingers, she took heart from the concerned look on his face. The AM-FM radio announced the 8:00 p.m. news summary. Too late for the library, which had cut back on its hours.

"Do you want to come out to my place for a drink instead?" Nicole searched for her purse.

"Maybe." Clark straightened the mess of papers on her desk.

"It was Raskin."

"What?"

"The nasty man in my dream."

Clark handed her the essay papers. "Let's get that drink."

CHAPTER 11

Before departing Minnesota, Nicole had splurged on three bottles of her favorite Cabernet Sauvignon in fear she would not find anything quite so elegant south of the border. She instructed Clark to sit on the porch swing and fetched two glasses of the wine. For a time, they sipped the Cabernet, savoring its earthy aromas and, without words, reveling in the evening. A full moon lit the lawn near the house with a strange but peaceful sheen of silver light. Clark lifted his glass to the moon, turning its contents slowly.

"I should quote you a love sonnet."

Nicole wondered if she should play the Elizabethan coquette in response to Clark's romantic overture. Should she, like one of those women in the romance novels, attempt to quell the heaving in her bodice? Instead, she gulped a good measure of her wine.

To hell with it. Nicole resolved to assert her rights as a modern woman. She took Clark's wineglass and set it next to hers on a small wicker table.

"Should I have forgone the sonnet and praised the wine?"

Nicole snaked her arm around Clark's neck and pulled him into a kiss. After surfacing from the first encounter, Nicole dove back for more, this time lightly nibbling on her partner's lower lip.

Unfortunately, what had proved in times past to be a reliable romantic gambit provoked only tragedy.

Munchkin took umbrage at watching the unseemly display of human passion and, after leaping to the back support of the swing, soared high in the air, landing claws-out on the back of Clark's neck.

"Aaaaahhh," Clark moaned, not in passion, but in pain from multiple wounds. The kitten's assault had forced the unfortunate man to pull away from Nicole's nibbling kiss, thus assuring him a punctured lower lip. A timely rescue from unbridled passion, perhaps, but the blood welling on Clark's lip seemed a high price to pay.

"Oh, Clark. I am so sorry." Nicole retreated to the kitchen for a towel and some ice. "Your lip looks very painful."

She fussed with the ice, pressing it to Clark's lip. Munchkin sat on the floor, tail swishing, eyes fixed on Clark's every movement. Any romantic plans for the evening had fizzled in the foregoing catastrophe.

Somewhat embarrassed yet still stirred by her part in the events that had unfolded, Nicole inventoried her patient's attractive features. Broad shoulders, a generous tousle of dark reddish-brown hair, a strong facial profile, and formerly, lips a woman would love to . . . nibble.

The ice reduced the swelling, and Clark thanked her for the "Foowence Naaghtingale thing." He picked up his glass of wine and carefully maneuvered the rim of his glass over the cut on his lower lip.

Keeping Munchkin in view as the kitten sank to the porch floor and rolled on her side, tail still in irritated motion, Clark volunteered to review what he'd found out listening to the tapes that afternoon.

With admirable diction, given the condition of his lip, Clark recounted the results of his latest visit to the university archives. He'd discovered that all but Professor Raskin's tape had deteriorated to the point where understanding proved impossible.

"But Professthor Waskins' tape ish werry clear."

Nicole dabbed more ice on Clark's lip before allowing him to continue. Munchkin lounged dangerously close to the wounded man's ankle.

Raskin's tape divulged several interesting facts and relationships from the university's past. According to the missing professor, DeTassell had convinced Raskin, Lazlo, Rubin, and Buster Melvin— members of the Kaliflower Kommune and Berkeley graduate students—that the future of the revolution would find seed in the fertile Iowa soil. There they would establish a university destined to topple the decaying institutions of American higher education, replacing them with a new "consciousness." The Kommune would use the substantial profits from its San Francisco operations and anticipated proceeds from future agricultural ventures in Iowa to fund their educational vision. DeTassell would continue to guide the group and planned to concentrate on business matters.

"Haf you ga a tape blayer," Clark asked, pressing his fingers against his puffy lip. He wanted Nicole to listen to part of the tape.

Nicole fetched the small boom box she kept in the kitchen. She also found some pain pills her dentist had prescribed after treating a gum infection. Clark gulped down a couple of pills with the rest of his wine, and dug out the Raskin tape from his pants' pocket.

But we should have known better than to trust Jimmy DeTassell. The first thing he does is to dump his girlfriend, and then we find out the young thing is pregnant. She was just a kid herself. Back then, Aurelia was . . . a beautiful girl. She should have taken the baby and gone somewhere away from all of us. As it was, DeTassell got his hooks in the boy, and the little snot is turning out just as bad as his father. Poor Aurelia's hooked up with Buster Melvin, and that'll lead to no good.

Nicole paused the tape. "This is incredible."

Clark nodded, settling back in a more comfortable position on the swing. Nicole started the tape again.

I shouldn't be saying this on tape, but what the hell. The original dream is gone. It was a pretty silly dream anyway. You ever read Hobbes, Montesquieu, and those boys? They had it right, human nature is corrupt, and we had a black-hearted bastard in our midst from the very start. Now the university will go down the drain. Just a matter of time. It's not about ideals; it's power and money now.

Clark took a deep breath and leaned forward. He looked very sleepy. "Tha's abow it."

"Are you OK?" Nicole held up the bottle of painkillers to check the recommended dose.

When she turned back to Clark, intending to warn him about drinking more wine with the pills, he'd already fallen asleep, his head thrown back and mouth wide open.

Munchkin vaulted up to his lap, curled in a tight ball, and began to purr.

CHAPTER 12

Professor Martin Dufer struggled with the focus knob on the old-fashioned overhead projector. The screen behind him displayed a block-lettered title: "Equality in Hiring."

"What? No colon?" Only a trace of Clark's lip injury remained after the holiday weekend.

Their departmental chairs had drafted Nicole and Clark to attend the faculty committee meeting on academic fairness. Not one of the tenured faculty in their departments had volunteered for the privilege. Given the myriad list of department, division, and college committees and task forces, Nicole couldn't much blame her colleagues for running and hiding, but she hoped not to abuse the power of her status if she ever joined the tenured ranks. She hated walking into a committee meeting inexperienced and knowing little or nothing about the topic at hand.

What sort of responsible representation could she offer for her department? As Bob Spiro, her department chair told her, "I'd go if I had the time, but it's really a matter of showing the departmental flag at these things. The dean keeps a scorecard, I think."

As far as Nicole could gather, Spiro spent most of his time trying to play politics and plot his climb to higher administrative positions within the university.

Clark, of course, had no choice but to agree his chairperson's request. He needed all the brownie points he could muster for his upcoming tenure decision. Not much freedom, academic or otherwise for someone in his shoes. At least that's how Nicole saw it.

Professor Dufer, a tenured member of the economics department, had the reputation as an articulate, steadfast conservative on most matters, and large numbers of students flocked to his classes on American government and politics. Nicole had glanced at a list of his publications and public presentations in an issue of the alumni magazine. No slacker was Dufer. He seemed to have earned a wary respect from the majority of faculty, even if they didn't much appreciate his personality.

Dufer had the unfortunate habit of speaking to his colleagues as if he were lecturing to a class of undergraduates. Nicole's ears already rang from the volume his voice produced throughout the conference room. She did her best to concentrate on the substance of his appeal for a "Humanities and Social Sciences Academic Equal Rights Statement."

"This is a key moment in the history of this college. The adoption of this statement as a principle for hiring, tenure, curriculum development, and our other faculty roles and responsibilities is absolutely critical." Dufer hooked his thumbs inside the leather suspenders stretching across his ample belly and surveyed the committee members seated around the conference table.

The professor pivoted to the side and made a sweeping gesture with his hand. "As you well know, faculty committees rarely meet in such grand surroundings as this . . . the DeTassell Foundation Conference Room. You should thus assume the president considers this statement a must in the agenda she has set forward in the Crisis Action plan."

"Does that mean we can use the executive toilets up here?"

An elderly man with huge reading glasses, erratic wisps of white hair sprouting from the sides of his head, and a complexion suitable for Madame Tussaud's museum sat facing Dufer. He wore a plastic name tag on his lapel from some long-past professional conference. It read, "Jerome Atrect—Geography."

"No, Jerry. Dammit. We talked about this yesterday." Dufer glared at the frail geographer.

Atrect retreated into the plush leather folds of his executive conference room chair.

"Colleagues, as you all should know, State Senator Tommy D. Stande has introduced a bill requesting all state-funded colleges and universities to adopt the Academic Equal Rights Act. Several state governments and the U.S. House of Representatives are moving in this bold direction as well." Dufer raised his voice another decibel. "I think it's time we protect students against political bias and enhance intellectual diversity on our campuses."

"Does this mean I have to go all the way down to the first floor?"

A vein pulsated wildly on Dufer's temple, and the look he gave Atrect would have reduced a lesser, or perhaps more complex, man to ashes. The woman next to Atrect whispered something in his ear. He excused himself and with mincing, stiff-kneed steps exited the room.

Several questions from the faculty diverted the further ascent of Dufer's blood pressure.

Nicole found the emerging debate fascinating, and Dufer seemed far more agile intellectually than she'd suspected as he faced an onslaught of tough questions. He parried any objection with a mantra honed to a fine edge: the Academic Equal Rights Act represented worthy and reasonable principles—scholarship over ideology, intellectual diversity, and the right of students not to suffer indoctrination from any professor, no matter what his political stripe.

"Why wouldn't we want to stand for these principles, my colleagues?" Dufer forced a smile worthy of any big-city ward heeler. "This is all about education, not indoctrination. Too long have our students been taught by liberal Democrats and 1960s radical leftists."

"Oh come on, Martin," one of the committee members complained. "What's your evidence?"

Dufer smiled at his questioner. Nicole guessed he had his guns loaded for this moment.

"Did you know that Democrats outnumber Republicans in academe by something like a seven-to-one margin? Is that balanced and fair? How many have heard of the students forced to write an essay on this topic: 'Why George Bush Is a War Criminal'? Is that balanced and fair? Did you know a professor in a prominent university told a student she'd have to drop his class for missing an hour's lecture to attend a conference for conservatives? Is that balanced and fair?"

Nicole whispered to Clark, "What is this . . . a white man's call and shout?"

Dufer made a show of counting the faculty attending the committee meeting. "My guess is we have a huge plurality of liberal Democrats and worse in this room."

Sachiko Matsuda, from cultural studies, waved her hand to be recognized. "Let me pose a theoretical question."

Jerry Atrect chose that moment to reenter the conference room. He smiled at Matsuda and apologized for interrupting. Squishing into the leather chair, he placed a plastic packet of candy on the table and struggled to tear it open. He succeeded only in spilling gummy red, green, and yellow candy pieces shaped like bears on the table. He offered to share with the woman sitting next to him.

"I've never tried these," he said to her. "The students seem to like them."

Dufer watched his nemesis divide the candies into color groups.

"In the wake of 9/11," said Matsuda, herself momentarily distracted by Atrect's Gummy Bear platoons, "a foremost conservative religious figure asserted that liberal civil liberties groups, feminists, homosexuals, and abortion rights supporters were partially responsible for the terrorist attacks. According to this good reverend, these groups had somehow made God angry with Americans. Given this person's huge influence and constituency, even at this university, does this mean I must leaven my classes with conservative opinions the likes of his?"

Before he could answer Matsuda's challenge, voices sounded from all angles, peppering Dufer with a crossfire of questions.

"Aren't you mandating some sort of artificially constructed balance of intellectual views? Will I be put on trial by students if I select one textbook over another? Isn't this the same sort of relativistic thinking and government intrusion conservatives want to avoid? Why limit it to the social sciences and the humanities? How about science? Or business administration? Won't students take all this the wrong way and twist it to influence grading and classroom assignments?"

Matsuda waited for the faculty's third degree to end, adding another question to the pile. "Isn't this simply an impossible model for any institution to follow?"

Dufer seemed unshaken by the committee's reaction, and threw a question back at his antagonists. "Do any of you, in all fairness, deny we have a problem?"

As he raised a declamatory fist in the air, readying another offensive, a choking cry of distress split the air.

"Aaaarrgh."

Eyes bulging and arms flapping, Atrect performed an odd, tormented dance, advancing by jerks and quivers to the front of the room. Bits of half-masticated candy bears hung like drowning sailors from the corners of his mouth.

"Jesus, Jerry!" Dufer wailed.

Clark bounded after the choking man, catching him at the overhead projector, maneuvering him for the necessary abdominal thrust.

"Bleeetchhuh."

Nicole and the committee members watched horror-struck as Atrect expelled a multicolored glop of candy on the hot glass surface of the overhead projector. The gummy mess sizzled and expanded, spilling down the sides of the machine.

Matsuda stood next to Nicole. "A strange explication of diversity, neh?"

In the aftermath of disaster, the faculty raced to finish the important business at hand—minus the unfortunate Professor Atrect, now on his way to the campus medical center.

Martin Dufer sat to the side of the room slumped and brooding, his overheads in a neglected pile near his chair. After a moment, he lumbered to his feet and left the meeting, his footsteps impeded, but slightly, by a yellow Gummy Bear flattened against the heel of his shoe.

Sunny Wriston, who taught family counseling and had her own local television hour on conflict management, watched the former committee chair exit the room. She tapped her knuckles for attention on the white board.

"Fellow committee members . . . gentle friends . . . can we please come to order," said Wriston. "Despite the disruption we've experienced, we still have twenty minutes remaining. I'd like to discuss something with you."

Without skipping a beat, Wriston floated from one committee member to another, distributing a beige handout labeled, "Commitment to and Expectations of Students."

"I demand a colon," said Clark.

An advisor to many admirable student groups on campus, Wriston urged the committee members to take a few minutes to study the handout.

"But before you do," she managed to spread her smile to even the most resistant onlooker. "Let's pause for a minute and take a deep breath."

"Breathe deeply. Go to that special place," she soothed, her eyes glowing. "That's it, close your eyes. Find your bliss."

"I'll take mine shaken, not stirred," said Clark, eyes shut, hands outstretched. "Two olives, please."

"What in the world is the point of this document, Sunny?"

Haskell Simon, a colleague of Roger Cantwell's in political science, wasted no time in registering his objections. "I don't like the direction it takes. Smacks of insane coddling to me. Where did you come up with this froth?"

"It's simply an issue of fairness, Haskell." Sunny walked behind Simon's chair and placed her hands on his shoulders. "As you know, many of us ask students to honor certain codes of conduct and responsibilities in our classes. For example, I think you have your students sign a pledge about plagiarism, don't you?"

Simon squirmed under her touch, but answered yes to Wriston's question.

The petite conflict manager winked at the others in the room and leaned down so that she and Simon were almost cheek to cheek. "We should have promises to keep, too. Now shouldn't we, Haskell?"

"Hogwash." Simon leaned away from Sunny, glaring at her. Nicole sensed that something more than professional disagreements had set this pair at odds with one another.

"I like it," said Clark. "I think this proposal recognizes that students and faculty are travelers on the same road. Both sides have necessary responsibilities to make sure the educational journey turns out right."

"With due regard for your inspiring metaphor, young man, I don't regard the teaching-learning process as one meriting such a grant of equality," Simon's eyebrows arched, and he addressed his next comment to Sunny Wriston. "What's next? Students lending their expertise for faculty government?"

Clark's stand on the issue impressed Nicole, but she worried he might end up offending someone on his tenure committee.

Matsuda raised her copy of the proposal. "I like the ideal expressed, but couldn't something like this lead to a host of much more legalistic rights and responsibilities? I'd hate to give some disaffected students and parents with access to litigious lawyers more chances to pounce on our university."

"But don't we have to operate according to some code as educators?" Clark pressed his case. "What does it imply to be a professional in higher education? I'd like a better road map. It would be good for students and their parents to see we take ourselves seriously as professionals."

"Maybe we would earn more respect," Sunny added, with a smile directed at Haskell Simon.

"I'd like to see if we could agree on a basic list of professional commitments we could make public for students. It ought to work both ways," said Clark. "Since we want to have students abide by a code of conduct and course contracts, don't we? Maybe they would take things more to heart if we did our part."

Simon rolled his eyes, appealing to others near him in mock desperation. "I pledge to my students a love feast of intellectual sharing and enduring, unfailing respect for their undiscovered genius. Yada yada yada. Ding ding ding. Spare me. Please."

Professor Ernst Flavelich, a quiet, circumspect plant physiologist, ignored Simon's display. "I'm not anxious to construct a long list of professional principles and responsibilities. That might be dangerous, and certainly it would be foolhardy. However, at the least, we should make some attempt at listing professional obligations—*specific* to our educational interactions with students. Just in our classroom relationship, what are our commitments to students who spend the semester with us? It's not a bad idea to set an example of such professional standards for our students."

"Shouldn't such a list include our advising roles?" asked a committee member. "Ernst, what about enforcing violations? I don't see how any of this makes sense without penalties," said Matsuda.

"This is something the whole faculty must consider."

Simon snatched up his notes, glaring at his colleagues.

Quickly the discussion advanced to intricate arguments about morality, orality, fatality, semiotics, linguistics, ballistics, structuralism, objectivism, yogi-isms, reification, sublation, globalization, and Oprah. Professor Flavelich stared at the opposite wall, his eyes glazed.

Nicole nudged Clark, and they prepared to leave as Wriston and Simon launched into a no-holds-barred shouting match.

As they exited the conference room, Clark told Nicole he'd drop by her office later that afternoon after he did some more research at the library archives.

"Let's eat over at my place tonight," he said.

Once back at her office building, Nicole stopped by the mailroom to see if any publishers had sent her exam copies of textbooks. Instead, she found a red envelope protruding from her mailbox slot. She popped open the wax seal to find a party invitation.

You and a significant other of your choice are invited to the 24th Annual DeTasselling Party on Friday, 11/1. Costumes are mandatory for this grand occasion.

Cocktails at 7 p.m.
R.S.V.P. Regrets Only. James and Ingrid DeTassell.

CHAPTER 13

At this point in the semester, Nicole found little time left for anything but preparing classes, grading papers, and meeting with students—most now terribly concerned about their grades.

Clark had those duties, too, plus the additional burden of preparing a thick application for his upcoming tenure review. Nicole thought the DeTassell party would be a good chance for them to let off some steam.

Clark had never attended the gala event because of his friendship with Rubin Leary. Rubin had railed fiercely against the party—"a frivolous exercise for the academic petty bourgeoisie"—and the hosts—"capitalist sellouts, exploiters, Corn Belt aristocrats." But this year, love triumphed over politics, and although Clark no longer received an invite because of his previous absences, he decided to accompany Nicole as a significant other.

He was especially enthused by his "significant other" designation. "Is it like going steady? Is there a special costume to wear?"

"Not until after the party," said Nicole.

Meanwhile, the faculty waged a valiant fight to register their opinions on the president's Crisis Action plan, but the stresses of midsemester sabotaged the best of intentions. Attendance at forums plunged, meeting cancellations multiplied, and intrafaculty squabbling prevailed.

Only the potential changes suggested for the core curriculum still excited the faculty. At a raucous session early in the week, a divided assembly of professors, tired and bitter after two hours of posturing and bickering, agreed on one thing—to postpone further discussion. They spent another long hour attempting to write a forceful letter to the president in favor of the postponement.

The spectacle of so many educated people attempting to write a simple paragraph amazed and dismayed Nicole, especially when the placement of a comma ignited an argument between professors of literature and communications.

As Clark observed of the final product, "Never have so many written so much without making any sense."

"Can anyone spell 'D-Y-S-F-U-N-C-T-I-O-N-A-L?'" Nicole wondered aloud.

The continuing disruptions among the faculty had her reeling, and the truculent ending of the faculty meeting on academic fairness had left its mark.

The majority of faculty seemed to have spun out of control, lurching every which way, given in to cynical games and ridiculous wrangling for power. How had so many apparently lost track of their better selves? Nicole could see herself falling down the same hole—losing her ideals about a life of college teaching and making a difference with students. Maybe she already had? Someone far better than she would find it hard holding on to dreams in the academic banana republic of Higher State.

Nicole thought it must be like this, though certainly to a smaller degree, at most any campus. How did faculty and administrators manage to hide this smarmy side from the students? Or did they? She remembered her fair share of burned-out idealists and tightly wound, remote faculty from her undergraduate classrooms. As much as she liked Rubin, and could imagine what he might have been as a teacher, Nicole now saw a man preoccupied with political battles. Maybe she was wrong. She hoped so.

How could professors teach students "what they might be" with any hope of success? Could any professor separate the sacred from the profane sides of their professional lives? How did some faculty at Higher State keep from falling into the pathological swamp? *Why am I obsessing about all of this when I have thirty essays to grade?*

Nicole could only guess at answers.

While the faculty fought each other and their own inner devils, Dr. Raskin's disappearance remained unexplained, and Higher State's "missing professor" had faded from the local TV news. Not many on the campus seemed to care much.

Clark had no time to dig around in the archives, but he did ask Polly to search for leads. Both Nicole and Clark were dying to learn more about the tangled past relationships of the university's founders.

Felton Bernswaggle, who seemed to know a hell of a lot about everything, except philosophy, informed Nicole that Detective Snife no longer considered Raskin's disappearance an active investigation. "Snife thinks the old codger may have manufactured the whole thing to dodge taxes or something."

"You seem so well informed," said Nicole. "Tell me what you know about Ingrid DeTassell."

"Ah. The mystery lady of the DeTassell Estate." Bernswaggle checked the immediate vicinity to see if anyone could overhear.

"Give, Felton. What about her?"

"Honestly, all I know is she dumped Raskin way back when and moved into James DeTassell's digs. From that time on she's been the Greta Garbo of the Heartland. She makes a public appearance every so often, but no one gets close to her."

Bernswaggle scampered away to huddle with the department secretary for a brief, whispered conversation. Nicole took a cup of coffee back to her office.

She clicked on her e-mail and found fifty-two unopened messages. Most seemed worthless, except for one she almost deleted—a day-old message from Aurelia Castle. Shouldn't that carry a virus alert?

Dean Melvin hadn't come up with any new assignments to burden Nicole recently. Even the "Push the Pedagogy" group languished as the demands of teaching and grading shifted into high gear. I don't have time for anything new, thought Nicole. Don't they have someone else to do all this crap?

She clicked open the message.

From: Aurelia Castle
Subject: Dean's Request
Nicole: Dean Melvin requests you contact Professor Lenore Sedgwick (Biology 7–3321, SB 314) immediately. She needs to talk with one of our new faculty members about participating in the "Scholarship of Teaching and Learning" group next semester.

Nicole quelled the urge to rip her computer terminal from its moorings and smash it to the floor. Instead, she imagined the pleasure she'd take in tying a double knot with Aurelia's long legs—all six of them.

"I do not have time for this," she informed her Bart Simpson head-knocker doll, and nudged the toy with her finger. "I knew you'd say that."

"Professor Sedgwick?" Nicole peeped through the open door leading into a single-office space. A small woman hunched over a long table overflowing with papers and computer printouts. She looked up for an instant and motioned Nicole to enter.

"I'll be done with this paragraph in a minute."

Nicole sat on a wooden chair with a Latin inscription and the official seal of some university. She watched Lenore Sedgwick pore over what seemed to be a scientific paper. The biologist smoothed an unruly cowlick at odds with her closely cropped gray hair. She tapped her foot in a rapid rhythm against the table leg.

At last Lenore pushed her reading aside. "I'm so sorry to keep you waiting. You must be Nicole Adams."

After some small talk, Lenore got right to business. "We are starting on the second semester of our scholarship of teaching and learning initiative. Dean Melvin thought you might be a good candidate for our discussion and research group. Are you familiar with the scholarship of teaching and learning?"

Nicole had determined not to commit any time to new committees, initiatives, projects, or groups—no matter what Dean Melvin might do. Lenore seemed like a very nice person, and maybe this scholarship of teaching and learning thing might be fun, but—no way.

"I guess your answer is no?" Lenore offered her a Fig Newton from a package on her desk. Nicole declined.

"Can you tell me something more about it?" Nicole had a vague idea about the scholarship of teaching and learning.

"It's somewhat of a difficult concept to explain at this stage." Sedgwick searched on the overloaded table, handing across a bibliographical listing of five pages. "As you can see, it keeps evolving and growing."

Nicole took a minute to scan the pages listing articles, books, conference reports, and Web sites. It surprised her how much attention the subject had garnered.

"Let's start this way," Lenore motioned for Nicole to pull her chair around and sit next to her. She cleared a space on the table and placed a long blank sheet of paper before them. "If we imagine this to be the landscape of scholarship in higher education, how many types of scholarship might we find?

"Does it make a difference what discipline one represents?"

"I don't think so. At least not as far as the general types of scholarship and what's characteristic of each."

She drew three signposts on the paper and labeled them "Scholarship of *Discovery* (basic research and investigation)," "Scholarship of *Application* (drawing together, making connections, context)," and "Scholarship of *Integration* (linking expertise and problem solving off campus)."

"I remember this from our grad assistant training seminar," said Nicole. "It's Boyer's *Scholarship Reconsidered*, isn't it? He said teaching is a form of scholarship . . . said he wanted to get away from teaching versus research dichotomy."

Nicole picked up a pencil from the desk and drew in another picket sign for "*Teaching*." She also connected the four picket signs with a line.

"I think Boyer said all of these 'scholarships' might be distinct, but they're interrelated, right?"

"Good memory," said Lenore. "Boyer's idea kicked up quite a surge of activity about teaching and, among other things, got the ball rolling for defining and developing a scholarship of teaching."

"I thought you called it the scholarship of teaching and learning."

"We do."

Lenore explained that those involved in the emerging movement recognized a need to link the two scholarships. One without the other didn't make sense. "We have to see how we are teaching and how our students are learning. As the experts put it, the 'character and depth' of students' learning."

Lenore excused herself to answer a phone call from her daughter, attempting to convince the teenager she could wear last winter's coat for another season. Nicole pretended to examine the bibliography.

On the surface, what Lenore had described and what Nicole knew about the scholarship of teaching and learning seemed attractive and reasonable. But Nicole needed a better definition, and she suspected so too did the majority of professors and academic officers in higher education.

How widespread and how accepted was this sort of scholarship? Wasn't it like educational research? If so, wouldn't you need to learn about educational psychology and statistical research at a fairly high level?

Who would have the time to do that and ignore research in their discipline?

Nicole didn't imagine the philosophy department would find anything but research and publication in the discipline credible. Would others contrast this sort of scholarship with what even she considered to be "real" research? Why would someone serious about philosophy or her disciplinary home get involved in scholarship that seemed peripheral? She could just imagine her graduate professor's reaction to the scholarship of teaching and learning.

"Don't ever have children," said Lenore, concluding a losing battle with her daughter.

"Or let them grow up to be teenagers?"

"Exactly."

Lenore fussed with the mess of papers and books on the table. She paused to look at Nicole. "I bet your asking yourself a lot of questions about the scholarship of teaching and learning."

Nicole nodded. "I'm not sure it's the thing for me right now."

"It can be quite a commitment to join our group and get involved in research. I'm spending way too much time trying to figure how students should be included in what we're doing."

"You mean permission to do research with them as subjects?"

Lenore sighed. "That and a ton of other issues. Just as an example, will using the classroom as a site of research threaten the learning process?" She glanced at Nicole, "There's more, if you want me to go on."

Before Nicole could answer, another professor appeared at the door to Lenore's office.

"Oh, Bernie . . . hello." Lenore greeted Bernie Bierman, one of her department colleagues, with a warm handshake and introduced him to Nicole. He gave Nicole an obligatory smile and declined Lenore's offer to make him some tea. Nicole sensed the man was up to something. She could taste the tension in the room and stayed alert for her chance to escape. Bierman maneuvered in the crowded office to stand near a four-drawer filing cabinet. The late afternoon sun poured over his shoulder. With his full beard and craggy brows, he reminded Nicole of a biblical prophet. One of the scary ones.

"Well, Lenore, what's the latest line on collaborative learning and reforming the lecture? Or is that reforming the lecturer?" Bierman acted like he needed a fight about something.

"Have you seen the latest issue of *Change*?" asked Lenore, squinting up at Bierman from her desk chair. "It has a wonderful article on the scholarship of teaching and learning."

Nicole wanted to shake Lenore and tell her not to go there. Talk about asking for trouble.

Bierman regarded Lenore as if she'd invited him to a Sex Pistols concert. A shade of purple worked its way over his cheekbones. Apparently Lenore had no fear, or she didn't know when to quit.

"Have you considered attending this fall's first workshop?" she asked.

"Lenore," Bierman sputtered despite himself, "I congratulate you on your recent success in funding, but I profoundly disagree with this

. . . teaching scholarship business. It's fine if you and your friends wish to discuss, shall we say, the nuts and bolts of teaching. However, good teaching is far more than applying some simplistic formulas and games to the classroom. Good teaching and scholarship in one's discipline are inextricably linked. Inextricably!"

"I don't disagree at all with the link you emphasize, but please come to the workshop and discuss your opinions," Lenore said.

Big mistake, thought Nicole.

Bierman snatched one of Lenore's journals off the shelf, a pleasant but subversive smile lurking on his face. He ticked off research article titles in the table of contents. "This is recognizable and defensible scholarship, Lenore. The other is all rhetoric at this point compared to the scholarship I know."

Flipping the journal back on the shelf, Bierman stood near Lenore, smiling down at her. "How will I know this scholarship of teaching when I see it? What makes it comparable to what scholars do in scientific disciplines?"

Nicole figured the embattled Lenore would like to smack Bierman upside the head with the latest hardcover biology text. But from what she'd told Nicole before Bierman showed up, the scholarship of teaching and learning as a field hadn't reached maturity. The converted still had to think about how to best "narrate" their work to people like Bierman, and Nicole had her questions and doubts as well.

Nicole watched Bierman as he leaned back against the file cabinet. She could see the wheels spinning, and she dreaded what the outcome would mean for Lenore.

"I accept your invitation for the fall workshop," said Bierman, his face flushed with delight at his decision.

Lenore smiled bravely.

Bierman paused as he reached the office door. "Lenore, would it be too much bother to make room for some others who . . . let's see . . . share my qualms about your scholarship of teaching and learning hypothesis?"

"Of course not." Lenore struggled to put forward a brave front.

CHAPTER 14

On the afternoon of the DeTassell party, Nicole and Munchkin lounged on the back patio of her rented house. Classes had ended at noon to allow students and faculty an extra half day of vacation.

On the twelve-by-twelve cement slab patio, she had assembled an odd group of chairs, a wooden picnic table, and two steel washing tubs filled with flowers she'd purchased at the garden and hardware store. The back patio's location shielded her from the prevailing prairie winds, now turned chilly in autumn. She and the cat soaked in the early afternoon sun, both near dozing in contentment.

Her cell phone chirped on the picnic table, sending Munchkin leaping to the patio concrete, hunched over, annoyed at the interruption. Nicole flicked open the cell phone. She knew it would be Clark, checking again to see if she needed anything at the store. They'd decided to throw a wine and cheese pre-party. Clark had turned out to be quite the detail man.

"Is it okay to invite Rubin?" asked Clark.

"He's welcome, of course." Nicole had indeed worried that Rubin would feel left out, despite all his ranting against the DeTassells.

"Great. I'll bring all the stuff we need in a couple of hours. Rubin can come with me."

"How will we get him home when it's time for the party?"

"Oh, don't worry. I think we've convinced him to go this year."

Before Nicole could ask more about Rubin's turnaround, Clark told her he'd explain later since he had arrived at the supermarket.

"Did you need crackers?"

"Yes, Clark. They're on the list under the cheese selections."

Munchkin lifted a paw for cleaning, blinking her eyes at Nicole from a new perch near the flowers.

"As Aeschylus informed us, kitty, 'The wisest of the wise may err.'"

Munchkin flopped on her side and probed a spider's web between the rungs of a chair.

By late afternoon, the wine and cheese pre-party had reached a fateful turning point.

"Should we open another bottle?" Clark asked, his eyes somewhat glassy.

Nicole looked from the kitchen window at her guests on the patio. Horace and Rubin laughed at something Sonja had said. Both men rocked back in their lawn chairs, teetering dangerously, their laughter loud and joyous. Hildie watched the men, tilting her wineglass for a long drink. She, too, caught a case of the giggles.

"It's only six o'clock. The party doesn't start till seven, and we've already knocked off three bottles," said Nicole. "We still have to get into our costumes."

Clark reached for a bottle of red wine. "In that case, we better open another bottle."

When the time came to depart for the DeTassell party, Nicole received an overwhelming vote of confidence as the designated driver. As she locked the front door, the others paraded to Hildie's Ford SUV, looking like refugees from a bad dream.

Hildie's costume transformed her into a Wagnerian opera diva. Sonja looked quite fetching as Barbie Doll meets Madonna. Horace had chosen a long, flowing robe and sandals to pose as Moses. He carried a cardboard tablet to solicit commandments from guests at the party. With a bit of borrowing from Rubin, Clark looked very much like a tall Austin Powers. He had overcooked the "Yeah, baby" line, but no one seemed to care. Nicole had resurrected a Parisian maid outfit she'd worn at a sorority party her freshman year in college. It still fit nicely, she thought.

The only fly in the ointment was Rubin. He'd arrived with no costume—though his everyday outfits may well have qualified—and insisted he needed something to serve as a complete disguise.

Horace and Sonja supplied a brilliant idea for Rubin's costume. He would go swathed in a super-size, green plastic garbage bag.

Horace cut some holes for feet in the bottom of the bag, and Rubin donned a pair of green kneesocks Nicole had found in her drawer. He already wore a nifty pair of lime green sneakers. Clark tied the open end of the bag over Rubin's head with a length of twine. Hildie suggested a flap for breathing and eating, as well as some pinholes to look through.

"What if I have to go to the can?" asked Rubin.

After a brief discussion among the costume designers, Horace took Rubin back into the kitchen. Nicole couldn't detect any alterations, but she assumed the problem had been solved.

Holding open the back door of the SUV for Rubin, Sonja said, "You look like a zucchini on steroids."

"Hell, Rubin," said Horace, admiring his handiwork, "all you have to do is lie on the floor and hope nobody wants you to pollinate."

They all piled into the SUV, careful not to, as Clark warned, "squash" Rubin in the backseat.

Nicole drove past the DeTassell Institute's front security gate and traveled west. Some five miles along the road, a fancy three-rail fence marked the beginning of the DeTassell estate. It took another mile, following the fence, before the Zucchini yawped and pointed to an open gate.

Nicole turned left on a gravel road, bordered on both sides by row upon row of pine trees. Cresting a hill, Nicole could see an enclave of several thatched-roof cottages and work buildings, dominated by what for all the world looked like an English country manor house.

Dozens of cars were parked in the circular driveway leading up to the DeTassell residence. Men and women dressed in a multiplicity of strange costumes, drank champagne from glass flutes, and nibbled on an array of appetizers borne by a fleet of waiters dressed in artistic tie-dyed shirts.

"The Zucchini informs me the Van Tassels have surpassed even his worst dreams about the triumph of free enterprise," said Clark.

"But the champagne looks mighty good." Horace popped open the door lock.

The friends advanced to the party with great excitement, followed by the lurching Zucchini.

"Yeah Baby!" Clark couldn't resist.

CHAPTER 15

Inside the DeTassell's manor, guests mingled throughout a spacious entry hall and a parlor dominated by a fireplace crafted from massive fieldstones. Men and women, busy gossiping and enjoying the party, hardly glanced at the strange ambulant Zucchini lumbering among them.

"The DeTassells are over there." Clark pointed to where the hosts, clad as ancient Roman nobility, stood by an ornate liquor cabinet and bar setup. Ingrid DeTassell's beauty, deepened by a scarlet stolla and palla, gave her an unmistakable advantage over any woman at the party.

Nicole spied Aurelia Castle in a distant corner of the room, eyes narrowed, sizing up the lady of the manor. As the Queen of Hearts, Aurelia dwarfed her escort, Dean Melvin, who looked uncomfortable in his guise as the White Rabbit. His furry white children's slippers did little to enhance his pose.

Hildie followed Nicole's gaze. "I can't believe Dean Melvin and Aurelia are at this party."

"He looks like Bugs Bunny," said Clark. "Something's afoot."

Rubin's muffled voice sounded from deep within his outfit. "Herd me in the direction of the serf's potty room will you, Hildie? I gotta go."

Nicole watched the pair navigate through the crowded room to a connecting hallway. They passed by Bob and Paula, dressed as Batman and Catwoman, standing near a small wine bar. Paula's costume clung to her body like snakeskin. Nicole had to admit, Bob cut a dashing figure in his Batman outfit, replete with a gold lamé utility belt and black codpiece.

Clark interrupted her reverie. "I bet it's padded," he said, pointing at the Caped Crusader's crotch.

Bob had seen the gesture and his eyes glared through the slits in his black cowl. He made an obscene gesture at Clark.

"I didn't know Ozzy Osbourne played Batman," said Nicole. Clark laughed and hugged her.

Horace and Sonja had commandeered chairs and a sofa outside the swirl of traffic, and Nicole and Clark joined their friends.

Following another round of champagne and scrumptious appetizers, two doors swung open at the end of the parlor, revealing a dining hall lit by glistening crystal chandeliers. A call to dine sounded, and guests funneled into the hall with great excitement.

Nicole, Clark, Horace, and Sonja, rejoined by Hildie and the Zucchini (now comfortably dehydrated) found a table with a view of the dais where the DeTassells and their guests of honor presided.

Halfway through the salad course, Horace grabbed one of the sharp knives from his place setting and hacked an armhole for Rubin. Feeding him the delightful spinach salad through his mouth slat had become a chore, and Rubin complained as balsamic dressing accumulated in drips sticking inside his costume. He spent the rest of the meal snaking a hairy arm out to seize choice bits of cuisine.

Sitting nearby, Corinne Runting said, "That thing's beginning to look like something out of a Japanese science fiction flick—a really bad one."

Rubin overheard the comment and made strange sucking sounds.

"Ross Perot's worst-case scenario." Runting edged her chair away from the Zucchini.

After the dinner plates had been cleared away and coffees, liqueurs, and desserts served, DeTassell pushed back his chair at the main table and stood before a speaker's podium draped in corn tassels. He welcomed all his guests and complimented them on their costumes.

A tall man, DeTassell had dark, wavy hair curling to the back of his collar. He matched his wife's beauty with a rugged handsomeness. It wasn't hard to imagine his charismatic power over lesser individuals, and Nicole saw how easily his guests fell under that spell.

"As you remember, our tradition at these gatherings is to enter into serious discussion about a key academic issue or trend." DeTassell smiled at the upturned faces in the audience. "Tonight's subject should light a spark in our proceedings. We shall discuss tenure."

The announcement drew a gasp from Clark and several other faculty members.

Just that morning, Clark had completed the finishing touches on his tenure book. He had worked hard at collecting evidence to impress his committee for more than six months. In a stout three-ring binder, with tabs for "teaching," "scholarship," and "service," he had inserted a proliferating mass of essays, syllabi, assignments, research articles, plans for future publications, reviews by outside experts, teaching evaluations, committee work reports, letters of recommendation, and just about anything that bore the slightest relationship to his quest. The tenure book and associated paperwork had grown to such proportions Clark now lugged it around in an airline case with wheels.

He gripped Nicole's hand tightly under the table with a sweaty palm as DeTassell introduced Ralph "Scooter" Humphries, a Des Moines Realtor and announced candidate for governor. Humphries served the voting district in the state senate. According to what Nicole understood, the politician had been under DeTassell's thumb for years. The locals held him up for ridicule, but he had risen to prominence throughout the state with DeTassell's money and skillful management.

Dressed in a politician's uniform—dark blue suit, vivid white shirt, red silk tie, and an American flag pin sparkling on his lapel—the aspiring gubernatorial nominee shook hands with everyone within his reach before he addressed the audience.

"My friends, as much as it pains me to tell you, the citizens of this fair state, at all social and economic levels, have a decidedly negative view of tenure. The farmers, small businessmen, and laborers of Iowa want an end to it. They don't have guaranteed job security. Why should you? The time is past due for substantive change, and we need to bring tuition-paying parents and civic and business leadership back on our side."

Clark sank lower in his chair, drumming his fingertips on the side of his face. Most others in the audience showed similar signs of distress at Humphries' attack on their time-honored institution.

"I hope he's just testing out this speech for the general voting public." Clark took down a good half glass of his wine. "We can trust a politician not to mean what he says, can't we?"

It would be six plus years before she *might* receive the protections tenure provided professors, so Nicole hadn't thought much about it. The nontenured folks, like herself, faced an immediate future in which you kept your mouth shut, worked like a dog, sucked up to tenured professors and administrators, lived in fear of bad student evaluations, and published as much as possible (most often before you had anything important to say). At the end of six years, you could apply for tenure and turn into a nervous wreck preparing all the materials. What a deal.

"Smart and talented people in my industry and others live by the rules of the marketplace. We ask for no special favors. We compete, but work together and stay accountable."

Scooter Humphries had hit his stride now, and he appeared undaunted challenging a hostile array of academics—many now sobering up from too much champagne and vintage wine selections. Nicole guessed Scooter didn't worry about losing votes among this constituency.

"Isn't our First Amendment protection sufficient for all Americans? Can't we strengthen such protections through enhanced contractual language? Why should professors need special treatment from the average citizen? Why should a small clique in today's professoriat enjoy an elite status now denied to the majority of nontenured and part-time faculty? Those good folks do most of the teaching and everyday work with the students, don't they?"

"He's going to talk about our 'customers' . . . I just know it," said Horace.

"We are talking about 'public' education, my friends." Humphries moved forward to the dance floor in front of the dais, "getting down" with his listeners. "Undergraduate students and the parents who support their children's educations are your customers . . ."

"Uh-huh. Oh baby. Do your thang, Scooter," Horace raised his wineglass in a toast to the speaker.

". . . and just like in my world, it's the satisfied and happy customers who pay the bills." Humphries paused to pour himself a glass of water. "The bottom line . . ."

"I knew it," Horace said, loudly enough to incite laughter from several tables nearby.

The laughing drew Humphries' attention, and he spoke directly to the smiling faces. "In the real world—and you should visit there some time—"

"Excuse me, Scooter." DeTassell tapped his knuckles on the podium. He walked over and stood in front of Humphries. Nicole felt a twinge of sympathy for the politician's embarrassment at being upstaged.

"I hate to interrupt your thought, Scooter," said DeTassell, with a quick wink at the audience, "but I think now might be a good time to ask our guests to launch the customary discussion period."

Humphries seemed resistant at first to DeTassell's suggestion, but he covered it well, smiling at his host and thanking the audience for their attention. Nicole watched him as he returned to his place at the dais. She thought poor Scooter looked more angry than crestfallen at losing his opportunity in the limelight.

"Man knows who pays the bills," Horace said.

"I'll weigh in at this point," said Roger Cantwell, decked out as an extra-large version of his hero, Theodore Roosevelt, replete with campaign hat, five-button khaki tunic, and leggings.

"The critical reality here is that tenure is a time-tested system allowing academics a bulwark against the dictates of the masses and the subversive unionism that threatens to invade and eviscerate the academic ideal."

Cantwell's defense of tenure drew applause from many of the faculty who rarely agreed with him.

"But make no mistake." Cantwell adjusted his Teddy Roosevelt glasses. "Tenure should not allow the introduction of controversial subject matter into classrooms unrelated to the subject being taught. Tenure has no place for activists who use the protection of academic freedom to propagandize."

Fellow Rough Rider Haskell Simon lurched to his feet, ready to support his leader. Unsteady after several glasses of wine and a good start into a bottle of Grand Marnier, Simon's lips moved but nothing came forth. A withering look from Cantwell warned against any further insubordination.

"I profoundly support academic freedom, but any award of tenure must be open to scrutiny," said Cantwell. "This business of keeping the tenure process secret—unrecorded and unavailable—allows for no oversight. The result? A serious lack of balance on our university faculty and a preponderance of one-sided liberal thinking in the classroom."

"Bully, Roger," chorused the Rough Riders, minus Simon, who slumped over his second helping of baked Alaska.

"Bull," screeched Alice Diugud, standing at a table behind Cantwell. "It's not about defending tenure in any framework—conservative or radical. In a time of impending financial ruin, we can't afford to keep the tenure system lock, stock, and barrel."

"But my dear Alice . . ." Cantwell attempted to regain the spotlight.

"Shut up, Roger." Diugud slammed down her wineglass, spattering the contents on the tablecloth. As the goddess Athena, she waved a wooden spear, menacing Cantwell, who had turned to confront her.

"We need options." Diugud had cowed the line of Rough Riders before her, though she kept her spear point dangerously near Cantwell's throat. "Why in a time of financial exigency should we keep deadwood who teach few and contribute little to university needs? Why, for heaven's sake, would you give tenure across the board to every field and discipline represented in a modern university? Turf Management? Industrial Hygiene? Fashion and Textile Design? Come on."

Nicole looked to see if Rubin might be ready to join the debate, but the Zucchini's chair stood empty. With the after-dinner discussion going full blast and tempers fraying, it seemed a perfect moment for a salvo from the feisty philosopher.

Sunny Wriston marched across the dining room to stand with Diugud. She wore a Little Bo Peep outfit, complete with lace bustier and bonnet. Nicole had seen the same outfit online at skimpyscantycostumes.com. Wriston pointed her shepherd's crook at a now resuscitated Simon's throat.

"We ought to be focused on how to realize our full potential as a university and educators." Wriston ignored Cantwell, glaring at Simon instead. "It's not about hanging on to a hundred-year-old dead horse."

Still smarting from their fight at the faculty committee meeting and, as Nicole would later learn, quite high on three glasses of Chardonnay, Wriston swung her crook at her hapless tormentor.

Simon pitched sideways to avoid the blow, knocking Cantwell off balance and careening into the row of Rough Riders. Theodore Roosevelt and his comrades fell down like dominoes.

"Historically this doesn't make any sense at all," said Clark, surveying the pileup. "I thought the charge went up the damn hill."

CHAPTER 16

Nicole watched in fascination as the arguments for and against tenure—as well as long-held personal vendettas—spilled out of control. Cantwell and the Rough Riders struggled to maintain ranks, and throughout the dining hall, guests broke into pockets of loud discussion and confrontation at close quarters.

Dean Melvin hopped into action, bounding around the room, imploring combatants to quell their fervor. In one dramatic moment, the White Rabbit separated a bogus Arnold Schwarzenegger from a mythological Hermaphroditus as the two wrestled near the dais.

Nicole and Clark stood at the back of the room, pressed against the wall, observing the mounting disorder.

"Look at DeTassell," Clark said. "He's loving all this."

DeTassell reclined in his chair, toying with a wineglass, smiling. He touched his wife's hand—a gesture of shared malevolence rather than affection.

Hildie rescued a glass of wine from a side table and swirled its contents, unconcerned about the disorder spreading across the dining hall. "It's like some sort of perverted team-building exercise. Who needs faculty retreats?"

At that instant, the Zucchini raced through the melee with Batman on his heels. The Zucchini put on the brakes, and as Batman flew by, swung what looked like a cylindrical map case at his pursuer's back, striking the superhero between the shoulders, sending him skidding across the floor headfirst where he lay writhing, whimpering, gagged by his cowl, his skintight Batman jersey and matching leotard bunched up, his cape torn and twisted—codpiece quite askew. Merely running through the scene in her mind made Nicole weary.

"Holy floor burns." Clark bent down to survey the damage. "Uncowl the poor fellow."

"Clark. This is serious." Nicole pealed back the Batmask.

"I'm hurt," bleated the Dark Knight, his mortification hanging from him like his codpiece. Clark and Nicole helped him to a sofa, where he moaned and rubbed his knees. Nicole turned back to scene in front of her. The Zucchini had charged the podium, and Ingrid DeTassell's beautiful lips curled in a scream at the bellicose vegetable's approach. The Zucchini launched at DeTassell.

Vegetable and host wrestled across platform—gourd and lord locked in mortal combat.

Only Horace's quick action saved the day. His robes flying behind him, he raced across a sea of combatants who separated before him. He pulled the Zucchini from his quarry and with the wiggling vegetable safely over his broad shoulder, Horace ran for the front door. Nicole, Clark, Hildie, and Sonja hurried after the fleeing pair.

"Stupid. Stupid," yelled the Zucchini. "Why did I do that?"

Despite his self-doubts, the Zucchini took a parting swing with his map case at Batman Bob Olufssen, who limped in pursuit, shouting obscenities. Map case met skinned knee with a resounding whack.

Over her shoulder, Nicole could see DeTassell yelling at Bob to continue his chase.

Once everyone had packed into Hildie's SUV, Nicole jammed it into all-wheel drive and powered through a hedge bordering the DeTassell's driveway.

She didn't have any other choice except that escape route, as too many vehicles crowded the circular driveway, and a polite exit didn't seem prudent, especially since a pair of muscular tie-dyed waiters had spotted the escapees.

With Hildie's operatic scream echoing through the vehicle's interior, Nicole jerked the steering wheel and accelerated across the vast front lawn.

"Head for that dirt road on the right," yelled Clark.

Wheels spinning, tearing up chunks of sod, Nicole steered by a formal rose garden, narrowly missing a gazebo and a sundial of wrought iron. The SUV went airborne as it raced over a knoll at the far edge of the lawn.

Hildie let loose a shriek worthy of a mezzo soprano in heat, truncated only by four wheels slapping down and grinding up the dirt road.

Nicole drove as fast as possible, dodging ruts and tree limbs jutting low over the darkened road. After two minutes of driving, she fishtailed onto a paved, single-lane road. She could see headlights in the distance and the welcome glow of an auto service plaza. They had emerged out of the woods on the backside of the DeTassell estate.

"Stop!" The order came from the rear seat where the Zucchini sat.

"Why? Let's get out of here." Clark half turned in the front seat to look at Rubin.

"I need to stop. Now."

Everyone piled out of the SUV and waited outside for Rubin, an action that later they could interpret only in terms of some weird group psychology—or, too many drinks. Instead of joining them outside the vehicle, Rubin clambered through the interior to the front seat. He locked the doors and fired up the engine.

"What are you doing, Rubin?" Horace pounded against the window. "You don't even have a driver's license."

The SUV shot away from the group, motor roaring, heading for the bright lights and the main road.

The strange and bedraggled crew left behind watched the retreating bulk of the SUV, the Zucchini's top barely visible through the rear window.

"We're all going to be unemployed by Monday morning," said Sonja, tugging off her Barbie Doll slippers, holding on to Horace's robe for balance.

"Yeah, baby," moaned Clark.

Nicole thought of all the work Clark had completed on his tenure application. She held close to him as they headed toward the service plaza.

The abandoned quintet spent the next hour drinking vending machine coffee, waiting for a taxi. Horace had a tough time convincing the lone taxi company in town to send a driver. The service plaza stood outside the city limits, and the dispatcher insisted on a jacked-up fare.

"When we get to my place, I'll make some decent coffee and we can have a late-night breakfast." Nicole hoped her offer of hospitality would brighten all their spirits.

"Can you scramble my eggs with ten aspirins?" Sonja massaged her temples.

"You got that right," said Horace. "What a party."

"Why would Rubin leave us stranded like this?" Hildie asked no one in particular.

For the remaining minutes before the taxi arrived, the group members relived the highlights of the DeTassell bash. Clark remained silent, perhaps fretting about the consequences of their high jinks.

Horace clapped him on the shoulder. "Come on, Clark. You're in the clear. I'll take the heat. What'll they do? Send me back to Georgetown?"

Clark's mood brightened somewhat, but he held tightly to Nicole's hand.

Following a short, but uncomfortable, ride packed into the town taxi—a Buick compact with shocks well past their prime—the group waited in Nicole's driveway while Horace paid the driver.

"It's about time you got here," someone yelled from the shadows of the front porch.

The glow of the taxi's headlights revealed Rubin Leary stepping off the porch to the front lawn, dressed not as a Zucchini, but wearing a rumpled dark suit and a starched, button-down shirt. Shoeless, feet squishing through the wet grass, Rubin moved across the lawn toward his friends. He wore a silk rep tie as a headband.

Nicole and Clark filled plates with scrambled eggs and toast as Rubin sat with the others around the kitchen table. The story he told had the ingredients for an epic tale, and he soaked in the attention of his listeners.

"I went to the bathroom again." Rubin pulled out several carved guest soaps from his pockets. "They had a ton of these sitting out for the taking. I got a bunch of little lotions and shampoos, too."

Hildie grabbed the ex-Zucchini's ear. "Rubin. Tell us what happened. Now."

Between bites of eggs and toast, Rubin explained his night's adventure.

After emptying the guest bathroom of useful sundries, he prowled through other rooms in the manor. Finding no additional treasure troves, he ventured out on the grounds in a nostalgic search for the first cottage constructed on the DeTassell acres. "I wanted to see the old place."

Rubin slurped the last of his coffee and looked at Clark for refill. "I stepped inside, and all of a sudden, somebody clobbers me with a pillowcase filled with corncobs."

Rubin rubbed the back of his head.

"I wake up ten minutes later with a lump on my noggin and wearing this goofy suit. The miserable sucker took my new Chucks, too." Rubin wiggled his toes for emphasis. "Somewhere there's a guy in my costume and with my rides."

"And he's driving my SUV," said Hildie.

"How did you get back here?" Nicole measured out more coffee grounds into the coffee machine basket.

"I made it out to the parking lot and found Haskell Simon trying to drive his car from the backseat. The crazy dude was drunk as an owl . . . kept going on about Sunny Wriston. I drove over here, and he headed off down the road. I got to get a license someday."

"The question is . . . who is this new Zucchini?" Horace looked around the table for answers to the mystery.

No one offered a guess.

After Nicole called the police to report the hijacking, a Normal police patrol spotted Hildie's vehicle near the campus, but no sign of the costumed car thief—the counterfeit Zucchini.

"I suspect we'd find someone dressed up like that." Detective Ron Snife had arrived within minutes after Nicole's missing vehicle report. He leaned up against the kitchen counter, scribbling on a hotel notepad Nicole had supplied him.

He examined the notepad and looked at Nicole, "Did you take the pen, too?"

The wall clock over the sink showed 4:00 a.m. and Nicole was in no mood for Snife's lame humor. She and the others wasted two hours explaining the attack on Rubin at the party and how that led to the SUV snatching. It seemed like Snife wrote his notes in slow motion and thought at the same speed.

Snife kept asking Rubin, "Why did you dress up like a Zucchini?"

Nicole guessed it was a logical question . . . once.

When the detective asked for details from the others, a tired and angry Rubin made soft "oinking" noises. Horace made him knock it off.

Snife didn't seem to notice, his attention riveted on the outfits Nicole and Sonja still wore.

At long last, the interrogation ended—the detective's store of stock questions exhausted, and his witnesses out of patience. The tipping point came when Nicole refused to make any more coffee.

"What am I? A damn Starbucks?"

After everyone had left the house, Nicole sat exhausted on her sofa. Only the promise of two more days away from work gave her any comfort. Monday would come soon enough, and she suspected it would be a day to forget.

CHAPTER 17

The Higher State University basketball team scored from all angles, tossing in three-pointers and banging home slam dunks against the team from Fargo Community College. Nicole and Clark cheered from the stands as the HSU "Torpids" scampered up and down the hardwood, overwhelming their opponents, who played like Canadian hockey players in silk shorts. Nicole assumed the nickname for Higher State's athletic teams was owed, once again, to the institution's twisted past. She couldn't wait to hear the fight song.

Most of the faculty turned out for the basketball game, despite the fact that few had yet recovered from the DeTassell's party and its tumultuous ending. Nicole noticed Haskell Simon sitting a couple of rows away in the bleachers. Only the bruises on his cheek and a robust hickey on his neck betrayed a partial reality of what had happened at the party's finale. According to Hildie, who called that afternoon, Sunny Wriston's well-aimed swat with her shepherd's crook had not prevented the two antagonists from later finding a . . . common ground. Hildie's source on the campus police revealed that a man garbed in an odd military outfit and a shepherdess with bustier and thong were detained in the campus sheep barns early Sunday morning.

The arresting officer, with admirable sensitivity, charged the pair with malicious mischief.

"Yow. Go Torpid." Clark joined the student cheering section in a team yell.

"That's Torpids, Clark."

"Not in the cheer."

Despite the exciting back-and-forth action of the game, Nicole thought about the many mysteries unsolved. Who had mugged Rubin and swiped his costume? What was the bogus Zucchini thinking when he hijacked the SUV? Why hadn't James DeTassell demanded a house-cleaning for what happened at the party? What sort of a mascot goes with a nickname like the "Torpids?"

"I don't think you can personify something like that." Clark had his mind on the basketball game.

Dean Melvin continued to haunt Nicole's life.

Perhaps it was retribution for her supporting role in the party's melt-down. More probably, Dean Melvin needed to reassert his administrative dominance. Rumor had it someone from religious studies —dressed as Elmer Fudd and chanting "hare, hare, hare"—grabbed Dean Melvin's bunny tail and hopped behind the embattled administrator as he attempted to restore order. Only a numbing right uppercut from Aurelia prevented further outrage. Whatever the motivation for his renewed exercise of authority, Dean Melvin zeroed in on Nicole for yet another unwanted assignment.

As a nod to her Lutheran grandmother in New Ulm, Minnesota, Nicole had decided to work in her office early Saturday afternoon—as atonement for *any* fault she bore for the events of the preceding evening. Within minutes of arriving at her office, she looked up from her desk, startled to see Aurelia looming over her.

"This is one of our targeted applications, and you are meeting him in ten minutes." The dean's handmaiden slapped an admissions file on Nicole's desk. "We want a hit on this one."

She flipped open the cover and pointed to the red, stamped letters on the student's application. "Read that."

"High Priority."

"Make it happen." Aurelia left without further instructions.

The applicant turned out to be the state's best basketball player, Jamal Walker. According to a note in his file, his mother and father worked in a small-town packing plant not far from Normal, and the young man wanted to attend school in Iowa so his parents could travel to the games.

"Any school in the state would want this kid," read the newspaper clipping of an interview with the Higher State University basketball coach. "He's an A student, too."

Nicole considered herself tall at five feet eight inches, but she had to crane her neck to greet Jamal. He seemed completely at ease with his height, smiling and greeting curious students as Nicole led him on a tour of the campus. Walking to the Bill Lee Athletic Complex, Jamal talked about his parents and the International Baccalaureate courses he had completed at his high school. No mention of basketball and his accomplishments in the sport. Nicole liked talking with him.

She decided to be direct. "Why do you want to go to college here?"

"I'm really not sure I want to go at all—anywhere." Jamal paused to look at the trophy case inside the athletic complex.

Nicole wanted to hear more, but standing under an atrium skylight in the shape of a huge basketball seemed at odds with serious conversation. A super-sized tableau of "Thunder Jam" Berkersen's basketball exploits—action photos, posters, game jerseys, bronzed size-18E basketball shoes—stretching across an entire wall didn't help either. Nicole suggested they visit the comfortable setting provided by the DeTassell Corn Products Alumni Lounge. The admissions director had plotted a map to guide Nicole's stint as a faculty "partner," and had given her a key to the lounge.

"Wow." Jamal took in the alumni digs with its plush chairs, extensive bar facilities, paneled walls, flat-screen TV monitors, and skyboxes with privacy glass exactly at midcourt for unobstructed spectator views of the basketball games.

Nicole examined stacks of personalized barware awaiting expensive beverages, marked with the names of well-heeled alumni. "You'd never have to think about a sweaty crowd of student fans up here."

"This is as gross as it gets." Jamal settled into one of the skybox chairs, and flipped the massage switch. "You gotta love it."

Nicole fiddled with the "BodyFit" controls built into her chair. "Tell me why you're unsure about going to college? Is it because of the recruiting pressure?"

"That's not it at all." Jamal's shoulders rolled slowly with the massage setting on his chair. "I can make more money now by turning pro. Why go to college and waste my best playing and earning years sitting in a classroom? All my friends are talking about college to get a good job. I can get a heck of a job without all the hassle."

Nicole waved goodbye in her head to all the economic arguments she'd read about the dollar rewards of a college education. This kid wasn't buying what most prospective students and their parents might.

"I've heard people talk about how they graduated with this and that major," said Jamal. "They didn't get the jobs they wanted even with their BA degrees. Now they complain about paying off student loans for the rest of their lives."

Nicole could understand that. Some of her college friends took graduate courses at night while working full-time. They learned a BA didn't guarantee promotions or management careers, especially with the proliferation of graduate degree programs around the country. She thought about the oversupply of graduate schools in her own field. Most of those grad students would be lucky to find a teaching job.

"It's possible a college experience means more than making money." Nicole hated to think somebody as young as Jamal would miss out on what she remembered about being an undergraduate. She could always come up with the usual list of reasons for going to college, but she didn't want to rely on boilerplate.

"My Dad never had the chance to go to college," Jamal said, "and he's worked hard all his life. Mom wanted to be a grade school teacher, and she's just now going back to school. I want to give my parents the things they deserve."

"What do they want for you?" Nicole thought about what her parents sacrificed to ensure her college education.

Jamal stood up, staring out at the empty arena. "They want me to get a college degree. I told them it shouldn't make any difference, but they're old-fashioned that way."

This young basketball star could probably go to college anywhere he wanted—on the basis of his academic talents. His skills on the court were a bonus. Nicole didn't need ACT scores and all the rest to convince her about Jamal's promise as a student.

But should Jamal end up at Higher State?

"I can learn a lot of things on my own. I don't need to be in a classroom."

"I'm sure you can, but you'll be missing so much."

"You keep saying that, but what is it I'll be missing?" Jamal turned away from the window and wandered over to a row of sports action photos on the side wall. "Don't give me that stuff about interacting with students from other backgrounds and cultures, either. What a crock. At every campus I visit, students only mix in classes or playing sports, and I'd have to live in the athletic dorm with all the other jocks. Have you noticed how every group here has its own spot in the cafeteria?"

"Sorry, but I'm no expert. I guess it's something students have to work out for themselves."

" 'It's not my job' . . . something like that?"

"I try to do my best for students in the classroom."

Nicole felt like she'd given the right answer, but it didn't sound like much.

"OK. Give me your best shot. If I picked Higher State, what can I expect as an intellectual payoff?" Jamal asked the question as if he didn't expect much for an answer. "I hope you can top what they told me yesterday down the road."

"What was that?" Nicole needed to organize her answer.

"The guy handed me this sheet from the College Board about *Why Get a College Degree.*" Jamal dug out a piece of paper printed off the Internet from his back pocket. "It promises all sorts of neat things . . . 'expand your knowledge and skills; express your thoughts clearly in speech and writing; increase your understanding of the world and community;' and 'grasp abstract concepts and thoughts.' "

Jamal passed the paper to Nicole. "Of course, it also says there are more jobs and more money for the price of a college degree."

"OK. But what's wrong with the things they've listed about college degrees and learning? You can't stand still at one level of ability and skills." Nicole assumed Jamal had more than an adequate start on the list he held. "For example, is the world going to be the same in ten or twenty years? Doesn't knowledge change pretty rapidly these days?"

Jamal sat in his chair again, searching for a new control setting. "Why will that make any difference to me? I'm going to be hooping it for a pro basketball team and taking care of my family."

"You'll never get injured and lose your career? Even if you might have some big self-insurance payoff, what would you do with your life? What happens when you're too old to keep playing?"

Jamal laughed. "I'll go back to school."

Nicole could see his point. Why should he go to school now? Adults went back to school all the time.

"I don't mean to hassle you, Professor Adams, but give me one good reason. I need to hear one."

"It doesn't work that way all the time. Good answers to important, complicated questions are always complex, and they can't be boiled down into a simple one or two points." Nicole worried she sounded like a lecture, and it wouldn't work to talk *at* Jamal. "Is that what you want?—a simple formula that doesn't do justice to your questions about going to college? You've asked a question I can't answer without taking some time to think, and you deserve an answer that fits who you are."

Jamal seemed wary, and Nicole knew he might judge her response as nothing more than an excuse. She didn't want him to walk away with that impression. "Would you be willing to give me a couple of days so I could write you what I think is a reasoned response to your question?"

She wanted him to attend college somewhere. "I'll write to you about why I want you to attend college—even if it isn't Higher State." Given what she knew about the university, she hoped it wouldn't be tops on his list.

"It's that important to you?" Jamal leaned back in his chair, regarding Nicole.

"It is."

"Fair enough, but answer me one last question." Jamal stood and watched out the skybox window at the prepractice gathering of basketball players on the floor below. "What made you all gung ho about college? What is this special thing about being a college student?"

Nicole struggled again to find the exactly the right answer. "I guess it was a professor I had as a sophomore. The class was a general education elective . . . a philosophy survey class. I really lucked out and had the discussion section taught by the professor."

Nicole had loved the lectures for the course. She delighted in following how the professor explained the most complex material and kept raising new questions, pushing for connections with her students' lives.

"I knew why my professor loved being a philosopher, and she made me want to find out so much more," said Nicole. "Somehow I felt it was important for me to be there for every class and to read beyond the assignments. Not because I wanted a good grade, but . . . it's hard to put this into words."

"You're doing pretty good so far," said Jamal.

Nicole tried to remember how she felt as a sophomore, so wrapped up in her favorite course. She guessed part of her excitement stemmed from her professor's obvious devotion to students. But it was more.

"One day, after my discussion section, I was walking back to my dorm. All the way back, I kept thinking about what we'd talked about and comparing that to my reading. Then I started making connections to my European history course and to what we'd been learning in biology . . . about the scientific method. In discussion, I'd even drawn a good parallel to one of Shakespeare's tragedies."

Nicole searched in a cooler built into the bar for something to drink. She found some water in plastic bottles and tossed one of them to Jamal. She figured the alumni didn't drink much water with all the fancy booze available for the games.

Jamal drank some water and waited for Nicole to continue her story.

At that moment, the padded doors opened at the far end of the room. A gorgeous African American student glided across the thick carpeting, long legs encased in sheer hose, providing a soft brushing percussion as she walked. A step behind came a blonde and a redhead dressed in the new cheerleader outfits donated by the Victoria's Secret outlet at the mall. A man dressed in a Higher State University warm-up suit, grinning like a used-car salesman, followed the trio far enough aft to appreciate their siren song.

"It's an integrated *Charlie's Angels*," Jamal muttered to Nicole. "I hate this part.""Sure you do," said Nicole. She didn't want to end their conversation, but even Jamal seemed eager to move on to the next phase of the recruiting process.

"Thanks for the time." Jamal smiled and reached to shake Nicole's hand. "I'll be eager to read your letter."

The students surrounded him, and the man in the warm-up suit stood next to Nicole. He gave her a quick pat on the back, his eyes appraising the basketball star and his admirers.

"Thanks a lot, professor. We'll take it from here."

CHAPTER 18

After Saturday's game, Nicole searched her desk for various position papers covering all sides of the upcoming debate on the core curriculum. Most of her weekend would be spent wading through the faculty rants on general education. The semester would come crashing to an end soon, and she had more than her share of work remaining.

Clark sat with his back to Nicole, contemplating Raskin's closet. He had located O'Callaghan's early architectural drawings for DeTassell Hall in the university archives that afternoon. Turning his attention to the heavy wooden bookcase adjacent to the closet, he tried to push it aside, but it wouldn't budge.

"What are you doing, Clark?"

Clark ignored her question and pulled out some of the books a few inches, peering into the space left behind. "Nothing unusual here."

"Why are you sniffing around the bookcase?"

"Because . . . I think we have a McGuffin."

"A what?"

"A false lead, mystery fans. According to the architectural drawings, there's a space behind the wall on this floor. My theory is . . . should you care to entertain it . . . O'Callaghan built this goofy closet to distract anybody looking for a hidden room."

"Why would he want to hide a room? It's so . . . academic novel."

Clark traced his finger across the books, pausing every so often to read the titles. He extracted a hardcover volume and flipped through the first few pages.

"Most of these are O'Callaghan's books." Clark handed *Frozen Splendor: An Architectural Tour of Fridley, Minnesota* to Nicole. "Look at the signature inside the cover."

Lazlo O'Callaghan had indeed penned his name.

"Rubin told me Lazlo and Raskin shared this office. I guess they were drinking buddies or something way back when." Clark knelt on one knee and examined a row of books on the far side of a lower shelf. "Now why would someone have these titles all neighborly like? Come here, Watson."

Nicole placed her hand on Clark's shoulder and snuggled down beside him. "Is that a new aftershave?"

"Please! We are in the midst of solving a mystery. Read these titles and cut that out."

"Who would write this stuff? *The Secret Door to Your Inner Chakras. Hidden Treasures of the Calvin Coolidge Art Collection. Disguising the Obvious: Effective Writing in Film Studies.*" Nicole turned her head sideways and read the last title in the row, "*Push and Shove: Memoirs of a Japanese Train Conductor.*"

"That's it." Clark pushed the closet door shut, placed his hand over the titles Nicole had read, and shoved them farther into the bookcase.

Nicole heard a soft click.

She stood to the side of the bookcase and gave it a nudge with her hip. It slid away on small parallel grooves neatly engineered in the floor. Where the bookcase had once stood, a darkened passageway led away from the office.

Clark stepped into the passage with Nicole clinging to his arm. "Let's see what we can see."

After a few steps, they bumped into another door. Clark took a deep breath and a firm grip on the door handle.

"Open Sesame. Go Torpid!" Clark yanked open the door.

They emerged into a sprawling loft space. The only light came from a small television set flickering in a dark corner.

Clark managed to find a switch on the wall, and a row of recessed floodlights illuminated a large room with a scattering of furniture and lamps. To the right, a tangle of easels, artist's brushes, and a rumpled canvas spread across a corner of the space. Tubes of paint, crumpled and dried up, littered the floor.

Across the loft space, on a large table, someone had been working with a utility razor knife, cutting out paintings and prints from their frames.

An old-fashioned Kelvinator refrigerator stood next to a paint-spattered sink, a round Formica table and two chairs close by. On the wall near the fridge hung a dusty wine rack with room for several bottles. Next to the wine rack, a small sketch, its edges yellowed with age, was tacked to the wall. The abstract style of an early O'Callaghan was unmistakable, and despite the enigmatic rendering, so too was the subject of the portrait—a young, raffish R. Reynolds Raskin.

Peeking through the opening of a thick, floor-to-ceiling damask curtain—stretching across an opposite corner of the loft—Nicole discovered the sleeping quarters. A queen-size mattress with rumpled spread and bedding took up most of the space. Strewn on the floor next to a cheap, unfinished wooden dresser lay strips of green plastic trash bags. The Zucchini had been here.

"Wow." Clark stood next to Nicole and looked beyond the curtain shielding the bedroom. He took in the Zucchini costume remains.

"OK," he spoke softly, "I think we have no choice but to call the indefatigable Detective Snife."

Before they left the secret loft space to make the call, Clark removed the sketch of Raskin from the wall. "No sense to leave it for the barbarians."

Ten minutes later, Detective Snife and a burly policeman arrived at the office. Snife ordered the policeman to stay with Nicole and Clark. He dashed through the opening into the loft space, returning after a few minutes, scratching his head.

"Looks like you two have been busy." Snife sat in Raskin's desk chair and gave Nicole the once-over—his opening gambit in what turned out to be a long interrogation. He treated Nicole and Clark as if they were burglary suspects.

Snife asked about anything and everything, but few questions seemed directly concerned with the discovery of the loft space. The detective spent considerable time making the two of them uncomfortable about their role in the DeTassell party meltdown. He also made some offhand, suggestive remarks about Nicole's relationship with Clark.

Clark asked Snife if he dated much. The detective told him to shut up.

Near midnight, Snife finally allowed Nicole and Clark to leave. He ordered one of the police officers to follow them back to Nicole's in his squad car.

Once at the house, Clark refused to leave Nicole alone. "I'll sleep here on the sofa tonight."

"Why?" She was pleased he would stay, but not necessarily about his gallantry.

Munchkin rubbed against Clark's leg, apparently happy to spend a night on the sofa with him.

"Something's not right."

"You don't trust our dear detective?"

"Hell, no."

They talked for a while about Raskin. All signs pointed to the missing professor as the man who'd mugged Rubin, stolen his costume, attacked DeTassell, and hijacked Hildie's SUV.

"Has he been hiding in that loft space?" Nicole handed Clark a sleeping bag and a pillow. "He must have cleaned out all of O'Callaghan's prints and paintings, don't you think?"

Clark plopped down on the sofa, burying his face in the pillow. "I hate mysteries."

"Poor baby."

"Do you have a night-light?"

"I guess so."

"Did you close the closet door?"

"Good night, Clark."

CHAPTER 19

"What the hell is this?" Horace Phillips examined a diagram jam-packed with arrows, boxes, and explanatory footnotes. "It looks like the playbook for the Harvard football team."

"I told you . . . it's the old requirements for our core curriculum compared with the dean's revised model." Rubin smiled at the befuddled faces staring at him around a table in the faculty dining room.

Draining the last of his raspberry iced tea and plucking a neglected pickle from Nicole's tuna salad plate, Rubin set off on a historical explanation of the core curriculum requirements.

"In a faraway kingdom, long ago . . . I guess it was the early 1990s . . . a committee of faculty at our great institution met at the academic roundtable to 'strengthen' general education standards and to 'better articulate the inherent, historic general education/liberal arts core of the undergraduate experience.'"

"Sounds familiar," said Horace. "It's like locusts, except general education reform comes more often."

His voice rising with excitement, Rubin described how the majority of the faculty representatives either knew nothing about the topic, didn't care, or championed the most conservative, traditional views.

The latter group, with support from most of the bystanders, cribbed ideas from the general education plans of heavyweight, prestigious institutions, constructing what they believed to be a new and unique "Core Curriculum."

"But it's not a core curriculum. It's a distribution model." Hildie drew her own diagram on the back of the original.

"Why not?" asked Nicole.

"A true core curriculum limits the number of courses, and faculty design those few to be wide ranging in subject and interdisciplinary."

"That's what I told them in so many words, but they didn't want to hear it." Rubin applied several layers of mustard to the hot dogs he'd brought with him from the student center grill. Nicole wondered what had happened to his support for the Young Militant Vegan Virgins?

Nicole enjoyed eating lunch in the faculty dining room. Normally, she couldn't afford it, but Dean Melvin had invited the whole faculty to a premeeting luncheon. The free food had drawn an overflow crowd, of course, and people sitting at neighboring tables couldn't help but eavesdrop on what Rubin had to say.

"Like a bunch of horse traders . . . maybe horse thieves . . . the faculty committee wrangled and swapped favors until everybody had a slice of the required credit pie, and that wouldn't be the last shovelful to hit the academic corral." Rubin turned to one of the eavesdroppers. "Am I mixing metaphors or something?"

"At any rate, when the smoke cleared, they had so many 'expressionary configurations,' 'expanding perspectives,' and 'channels of inquiry,' it takes students forever to complete the requirements."

"I'll bet most of the designers didn't want to teach the courses." Horace seemed to be enjoying the discussion. "I'll also bet most of those courses are taught by junior faculty and adjuncts, while the departments divide up the development money."

"Touché." Rubin smiled in appreciation at his friend. "Our departmental leaders showed 'em philosophers can count students too."

"Weren't you on the general education committee?" asked Hildie.

"Until they voted me off."

Rubin explained the causes of his dismissal, which boiled down to the fact he'd researched gen-ed plans from across the country, revealing that without the fancy catalog copy, Higher State's new version mirrored all the others—something the committee didn't want to hear. Using examples from the University of Wisconsin–Waunakee, Kansas State College of Fashion and Intelligent Design, Tai Kwon Do On-Line Chiropractic, Northeastern Idaho International, Alabama Aeronautical and Bible College ("Learn with a wing and a prayer"), and a host of other colleges and universities, he'd hammered home his point.

"That's when they threw me out." Rubin dabbed at a spot of mustard spreading near the logo on his polo shirt.

Nicole could tell he'd been shopping at the cut-rate outlet mall outside of town. His polo shirt had a huge collar and the sleeves barely reached past his armpits. The psychotic green color of the polo clashed with the brown logo, as well as the mustard stain. The tartan red and navy pants must have been the product of a shopping trip many years past.

"When it was all said and done, the faculty senate requested some minor alterations." Rubin rubbed at the mustard stain with a wet cloth napkin Nicole had offered him. "Lost to our educational history is the Transpersonal/Contemplative Well-Being channel of inquiry, and in Societal and Theological Truths, students may no longer substitute 'Introduction to Marketing' for 'Religions and World Cultures.'"

"So from what I can gather," Sonja said, handing Rubin another wet napkin, "the proposed new requirements for the core curriculum cuts down the modes and cleans up the courses."

Hildie found a sparkling soda on a drink tray near their table and set to the task of erasing Rubin's stain.

"Cut 'em and clean 'em. Just like a fish," said Rubin. Rubin waived what remained of his hotdog in the air to emphasize his point. Another glob of mustard plopped on his shirt collar.

Hildie threw down the napkin and drank the sparkling soda.

To Nicole, all the talk about general education, core curriculums, and obtuse designations for course requirements seemed . . . well . . . surreal.

She could still remember how little attention she and her friends as undergraduates paid to the rhetoric flying about in the university catalog about general education. She signed up for the right courses, piled up the credits, and fulfilled the requirements. To her, the debate about the core curriculum at Higher State was the perfect example of the ivory tower. A bunch of faculty sitting around arguing life and death about things they never shared with students . . . at least in a way the students could understand.

Nicole wondered exactly what did college students remember or possibly find useful from their undergraduate general education courses. Name an important poet and a novelist of the fin de siècle? Can you list the four basic forces of the universe? What is Gresham's law? Define the meaning of Occam's razor. What is the function of the pituitary gland? All things forgotten the minute after taking final exams—that's what general education meant to most undergraduates.

The professors dreaming up general education models made one huge mistake in Nicole's opinion. They expected the students to attain it by osmosis or something. She bet most undergraduates didn't get it . . . and didn't much care.

"So what's your plan for general education?" asked Nicole.

"I wish we could go back to the one we invented," said Rubin.

"You know that wouldn't work now." Hildie rolled her eyes as Rubin doctored up his final hot dog with more mustard. "We have too many students."

"What was the plan you invented?" asked Clark.

"It was a neat idea," said Hildie. "Every first-year student took a section of the 'Educated Person' course we'd designed, and almost all the faculty participated in the program some way."

"We team-taught the course," Rubin said, picking up the story, "and some of us prepared readings books and wrote essays. At the end of the semester, students had quite a few good ideas about an educated person. They were ready to map out their own general education requirements."

"How did that work?" Nicole found the approach intriguing. Here was a system that allowed students in on the issue of general education from the very beginning.

"At the end of the course, our students submitted their plans for general education to one of several faculty approval committees." Hildie explained that the faculty committees had agreed on general guidelines for the student plans. "For example, each plan had to have a minimum of forty-eight semester credits. If students didn't include some of the basic characteristics faculty had suggested about a well-rounded general education, they had to justify their choices and exclusions."

"Sounds interesting, but complicated. It must have meant a ton of work for faculty," said Horace. "Lots of negotiation . . . lots of persuasion."

"It was worth it," said Rubin softly. "The faculty and students ended up discussing and refining what it means to be an educated person every semester."

"Not a bad thing," said Horace.

"I can see some real advantages." Clark added some sweetener to his iced tea. "It had to fail, though. Didn't it?"

Rubin didn't respond.

Though Nicole had been thinking along the same lines as Clark, she wished he hadn't spoiled the discussion. She wanted to hear more of the details from Hildie and Rubin. As it turned out, Clark's interruption came right when Dean Melvin decided to open the meeting.

Poised behind a small lectern, Dean Melvin tapped for quiet on an empty glass. The faculty, busy eating and talking, paid no attention.

Aurelia stopped a passing waiter and snatched his empty metal serving plate. She crashed her knuckles against it and the sound rumbled throughout the dining area like a Chinese gong. In no time, Dean Melvin was droning down the highway of his opening remarks.

Given the weekend's events and dramatic outcome, Nicole found it hard to keep her mind on the topic at hand.

She and Clark had gone back to her office Sunday afternoon, hoping to spend more time sleuthing in the hidden loft space, but the foreman of a campus work crew barred their entrance to DeTassell Hall. As Clark tried to convince the foreman to let them enter the building, Nicole had observed several workers on a rig blowing insulation into the northeast corner of the third floor. Why the cover-up? Who had Detective Snife informed about the loft space? Better yet . . . who had ordered the cover-up?

When she returned to her office Monday morning, Nicole found another surprise. The bookcase in her office had been removed and the opening behind it walled shut. A busy night of construction work made it seem like Raskin's and O'Callaghan's hideaway had never existed. But she could picture the two of them, many years past, enjoying the secret of their loft space, the artist busy with his canvas and paints.

As far as Nicole could discern, the faculty had enclosed and hidden their memories of the DeTassell party. Before gathering for the lunch meeting, they had tended to business throughout Monday morning, tight-lipped, unwilling to breath the slightest word about the party's riotous climax. No one seemed to know about the postparty discovery of Raskin's lair. Nicole wondered who, if anyone, knew Raskin had reappeared from the ranks of the missing.

Thanks to a phone call from Polly the librarian they did learn something. Someone else had been busy investigating university history and construction plans for DeTassell Hall. Apparently, Bob Olufssen had reason to be in the library beyond seeking out the latest theories on foreign language instruction. The dean chattered on as Nicole struggled to concentrate on his presentation. He seemed to be warming up his motor for a stretch run. After a minute, he hit the gas and, in no uncertain terms, reminded faculty of the president's desire to better serve students, and thus increase enrollment.

"Let us move ahead. We are out of step with what is an essential general education for the twenty-first century targeted to our Higher State University students. We must reduce, not complicate the general education requirements embodied in the core curriculum."

Dean Melvin paused, allowing his warning to register with the faculty. "This doesn't mean, however, we should sacrifice our educational ideals and what we know is right. But to do nothing invites disaster—perhaps even the end of this university and our careers here."

Nicole glanced around the room. She had expected a real dogfight between the faculty and Dean Melvin—at least some hostile reaction to the message he now delivered. But most of the faculty had partaken extensively of the free lunch and slumped in their chairs, eyelids drooping.

Even the determined supporters of the core curriculum were without a leading voice.

The heart and soul of the status quo, Roger Cantwell, had not attended the meeting, remaining under his physician's care for a strained back suffered in the Rough Riders' synchronized pratfall. According to Felton Bernswaggle's post-party gossip, Martin Dufer had driven his car through a next-door neighbor's garage door upon returning to his housing development that fateful night. He would be tied up in insurance meetings all day. As for Haskell Simon, he sat close to Sunny Wriston in a dark corner of the dining room blissfully unaware of anything except his companion. At least the couple wore business clothes, though Nicole couldn't help but be reminded of their recent adventuring *en costume.*

"Before I continue," Dean Melvin sprouted a wide smile, "let me assure those of you waiting for our dessert. We have a special treat ready, but our chefs are a bit behind on the baking."

The dean whispered something to Aurelia, and she headed off toward the kitchen.

"In the early days of our university," Dean Melvin continued, "though flawed and helpless idealists we early pioneers were, we did discuss with sometimes alarming frequency and outsized emotion what we wanted students to gain from their undergraduate educations."

Dean Melvin walked to an open space next to the head table where he could see all the assembled faculty. "We constructed a wonderful approach to general education and to the overall liberal education of our students."

Hildie put her hand on Rubin's shoulder and gave him a look of amazement.

"Yet," Dean Melvin continued, deflating Hildie's expression, "even in the relatively short run of years between our founding and our present crisis, the world, higher education, and our students have changed significantly."

"Duh," said Horace.

"Same old, same old." Rubin slouched forward and nibbled on some potato chips remaining in the sack he'd bought from the grill.

"The general education revision I propose you adopt builds on our hopes for the future. It draws from our experience and ideals but looks forward with a clear-eyed, realistic vision."

Horace made a face and kneaded his stomach. "I'm not sure the dessert will be worth all this."

"Sure, go ahead and leave us here like lambs for the slaughter," said Hildie.

"Hey, I'm just a visiting professor." Horace smiled and rose to leave the table. The remaining others watched him with dismay.

"I'm just teasing." Horace sat down. "You think I'd miss dessert?"

CHAPTER 20

Dean Melvin paused in midsentence, tilted his head back, and inhaled deeply, his nose trained at the kitchen. "Doesn't that smell good?"

Led by Aurelia, a parade of student waiters burst through the kitchen's double doors. Each waiter carried a serving platter laden with cookies and brownies. They deposited the sugary treasures on the front table.

Faculty members streamed toward the baked goods from all four corners of the room without proper invitation and instructions.

Nicole suspected Aurelia would take decisive action. She did.

"Stop right where you are!" Aurelia shouted her warning at the advancing hordes, and deftly twisted the little finger of an offender reaching for a chocolate chip cookie. In her grasp, the academic danced like an Appalachian paddle puppet.

Aurelia's unrelenting stand on baked goods consumption won the day, and the sweet-deprived faculty returned to their seats. After a brief conference with the staff, Aurelia ordered them to bear small plates of cookies and brownies to each table. She made sure to divvy up but one cookie and one brownie per faculty member.

"These delicious treats are a special gift from the DeTassell Foundation and the staff at the institute. Enjoy," said Dean Melvin.

"Thank you so much, Aurelia." Dean Melvin beamed at his assistant as she handed him a plate with not one, but several cookies. She sat at the front table, crossed her legs, and nibbled on the edge of a white chocolate, macadamia nut cookie.

"She makes that look like something out of a foreign film," said Sonja.

The brownies looked absolutely scrumptious to Nicole, but she knew Clark loved fudge and chocolate. She resolved to eat only a raisin oatmeal cookie, and passed her brownie on to Clark.

As everyone settled back to enjoy their treats, Dean Melvin picked up the threads of his earlier address on general education. He talked about general education reform in higher education and related, emerging issues of assessment with much enthusiasm. From what Nicole could tell, Dean Melvin really knew his stuff.

He warned that, often as not, changes in the design of general education programs threatened to divide and embitter faculty and academic departments. Changes were also expensive to implement. Nicole found it interesting that the percentage allocated to general education in college curriculums had declined from above 45 percent to somewhere near 33 percent on average since the 1960s. If Nicole read it correctly, though, the dean's plan didn't improve on that lower percentage.

"So here's what we'll do." Dean Melvin requested Aurelia and Paula Prentiss to distribute the new general education requirements at Higher State. The two-page summary of the new requirements carried a substantial title: "Knowing, Mind-Setting, Doing, Daring, and Living: Skills, Attitudes, Actions, Risks, and Multicultural-Global-Lifelong Learning for the 21st Century."

"Remember, please." The dean waved his copy of the requirements in the air. "Whoever teaches in the general education program, and how he or she goes about that teaching, probably matters more than any ideal structure we approve."

Nicole felt that statement made good sense, but the faculty seemed not to pay much attention, concentrating on their cookies and brownies instead.

She glanced over at Rubin. He hunched forward in his chair, sketching on the tablecloth with great energy and concentration, drawing a series of geometric shapes with a ballpoint pen. Hildie watched his progress with equal focus.

Next to them, Horace poured a full glass of iced tea and drank it down. One of the ice cubes dropped through the open neck of his shirt. Horace and Sonja giggled.

"How long have we been here?" Clark studied his watch. "It seems like we just started, and it's already 2:00 p.m."

Dean Melvin didn't seem to mind the growing noise from conversation and activities at each of the tables. He took a small section of cookie and popped it into his mouth. "The proposal you have before you has four frameworks for the twenty-first century: basic literacy, technological literacy, visual literacy, and marketplace literacy. It has depth and breadth. It really beefs up our required courses for learning skills, like language and mathematics.

"Is he saying what I think he's saying?" Nicole looked to her friends for an answer. None was forthcoming. "This plan makes arts and sciences a junior partner in general education. We could lose a lot of courses."

Clark and Horace were acting like high-school halfwits, shooting grapes into a pitcher of water. Horace blocked Clark's grape, slapping it well across the room.

"Don't be bringing that stuff in my kitchen," said Horace.

Clark launched another grape. His shot plunked into the water, eluding Horace's attempt to block it. Clark pounded his chest and waggled his head back and forth, a grin of phony self-amazement plastered on his face. Nicole had seen the basketball players at the game do the same thing.

"Come on, you guys. What is going on?" Nicole cuffed Horace's grape aside as he tried another shot.

"Dog! That gal's got game." Horace said, trading a high-five with Clark. In a matter of minutes, the meeting had lurched out of control. Nicole couldn't believe the disorder spreading around her.

She watched for a reaction from Dean Melvin, but he bit into another cookie, chewing slowly and watching the strange scene unfolding before him. Aurelia poured him a glass of water and he whispered to her. She laughed and returned to her seat.

"I believe our general education plan should focus on sets of usable skills and understandings. It should not slight the vocational concerns of our students. Business administration, computer studies, and other similar areas should be an integral part of general education choices. If, as our accrediting association and other experts are correct," Dean Melvin curled his lip and raised an eyebrow as preface to his conclusion, "then our approach will be one that will mirror our institutional mission and best serve our students."

Nicole thought the Dean's words would now ignite a storm of reaction.

Nothing. To her dismay, Hildie, Horace, and Sonja were harmonizing softly to the chorus of the Beatle's *Let It Be*. Clark and Rubin played riffs on air guitars.

Nicole raised her hand to speak. Dean Melvin saw her signal, but ignored her. She went ahead anyway. "If we adopt your interpretation of general education, we'll surely threaten our accreditation. We'll lose students, not gain them."

Nicole had surprised herself by interrupting, but somebody needed to speak up.

"How will students learn about artistic creation?" asked Nicole. "How will these requirements expose students to the fundamental intellectual skills and methods represented by the arts and sciences?"

Dean Melvin took a step toward Nicole, folding his arms across his chest like a long-suffering parent. "It's simple. We can embed the arts and sciences throughout the general education curriculum."

"But Dean Melvin, you've listed course requirements like career exploration and 'Introduction to the Marketplace.' How do we embed the substance of our disciplines in courses like these?" Nicole could see only a minor voice for philosophy or the other liberal arts disciplines in any of the required courses.

"Let's not get bogged down in those details at this point. Besides, Nicole, one could argue that a course in statistics or marketing could easily advance the skills associated with the liberal arts. Problem solving? Posing good questions? Making connections? Don't forget how technical and narrowly focused philosophy or literature can be. It depends on how one teaches."

Dean Melvin turned away from Nicole, signaling an end to their conversation. "I thank Professor Adams for her remarks, but I think most of the faculty would like to end our meeting."

Apparently the dean had read the pulse of the faculty correctly. Throughout the room men and women dozed, stared into the distance, and smiled brightly for no apparent reason.

"I could go for some munchies," said Sonja, with more volume than she needed to be heard.

"Yeesss," said Horace, his eyes somewhat bloodshot. Others around the room also agreed with Horace.

As if on cue, Aurelia marched the waiters through the kitchen doors, their trays filled this time with fruits, nuts, and cheeses. Samovars filled with coffee and hot water for tea followed.

"While you enjoy these healthful snacks, let me say that I greatly appreciate your cooperation today." Dean Melvin's voice had acquired a gravitas that Nicole took as a hint the meeting would indeed conclude.

"We've made great progress in preserving and shaping the future of our university. President Monarck and I accept your approval of the new general education curriculum and the restructuring of the arts and sciences division. *Tende altius*, my friends and colleagues . . . *Tende altius*. Let us all reach higher."

Nicole's intended dissent to the dean's outrageous manipulation of the faculty process disintegrated to a gasp. At the entrance to the dining room stood none other than Professor R. Reynolds Raskin.

"You've really outdone yourself this time, Buster." Raskin advanced at Dean Melvin, who retreated to Aurelia's side. Aurelia seemed as dumbfounded as the dean.

Gubernatorial aspirant Scooter Humphries, flanked by several Iowa State Police officers, followed the once missing professor into the room.

"Folks, I hate to break into the dean's Land of Oz here, but the next governor of our fair state . . . my good friend . . . the estimable Scooter Humphries has some important announcements." Raskin waved Humphries forward and snatched a cookie off the plate once reserved for the dean.

CHAPTER 21

"It's a great pleasure to be with you once again . . . and so soon."
Scooter Humphries gave his tie knot a quick adjustment. Nicole appraised the double-breasted, gray pinstripe suit he wore. It fit him to perfection.

"I recognize several of you even without your costumes," said the politician, laughing and pointing at individuals around the room.

Most of the faculty, Nicole included, straightened in their chairs, assuming the ideal mien they envisioned for their students—attentive, respectful, ready to please.

"How did this guy turn up?" Clark seemed disoriented.

Horace reached for the water pitcher. "Why are all these grapes in here? I thought they used lemons."

The effects of what Nicole now recognized to be a very potent and unique strain of marijuana had vanished, but all who had eaten a brownie seemed to have no clear memory of their actions the previous hour. The altered structure of the marijuana—what Nicole imagined as a product of warped scientific minds within DeTassell's Institute for Organic Farming—apparently had the capability to yield a time-released high and to wipe out recall. Nicole figured Dean Melvin and

Aurelia had seized an opportunity to test this discovery as an academic management technique . . . "better curriculum through chemistry" as it were.

Humphries flashed a white-toothed smile at his audience. "I will be counting on the support of each and every one of you in next fall's election. It'll be a tough campaign and should come down to a few key voting districts. As this particular district goes, so will go my future."

Dean Melvin applauded much too eagerly, his eyes darted back and forth from Humphries to the faculty. Aurelia reached for a remaining brownie on the plate next to her.

"I have several important announcements for you today." Humphries linked arms with Raskin. "First, of course, we can welcome Dr. Raskin back to campus. He's had quite a run these past few weeks, and we are thrilled at his return."

Humphries drew Raskin forward and initiated a round of applause.

Raskin lowered his gaze, the slightest of smiles showing on his face.

"As a result of information supplied to us by Dr. Raskin," said Humphries, his jaw jutting, his voice filled with drama, "we have this morning arrested James DeTassell and several of his associates on criminal charges, including theft of precious works of art, the attempted kidnapping of Dr. Raskin, the production and sale of an illegal drug, and money laundering."

Humphries raised his hand to quiet the reaction of the faculty. "It is also our suspicion that James DeTassell, using his influential position on the Board of Seers, played a key role in pushing our beloved institution to the brink of financial ruin."

"Why?" yelled out Professor Matsuda.

"Why?" Humphries scowled at Matsuda, as if she couldn't grasp the obvious. "So he could return Higher State University to private status and launder his drug profits. DeTassell could use the cover of legitimate university fiscal operations once he had gained control."

Humphries remained quiet for a few seconds. His audience shifted uncomfortably, expecting more bad news. But a political plug was way past due. "As your future governor, you can take today's action as evidence of the fight I will wage against the wave of crime and corruption in our state."

"Have we moved to another state?" Rubin still seemed confused.

The faculty applauded the remainder of Humphries' political sound bites as best they could. From what Nicole could see, many gathered in the room had difficulty coordinating their hands to clap. The resulting applause sounded like a pack of dogs licking their nether parts.

Nicole paid little attention as Humphries launched further into his election speech, rambling on about how he had "a plan" and interspersing his remarks with something about "everyone knows it's hard work."

Making complete sense out of Raskin's reappearance and DeTassell's arrest still proved difficult for Nicole. Only after Humphries ended his spiel and made his next dramatic announcement did pieces of the puzzle better fit.

"Let me end my visit with another salute to the courageous and thoughtful man at my side." Humphries gripped Raskin's shoulder, admiration spread across his face. "As you may know, the artistic works of Dr. Raskin's great friend, companion, and colleague, the late Lazlo O'Callaghan, recently have achieved a well-deserved, worldwide prominence. The prices art collectors are now willing to pay for an O'Callaghan have gone through the ceiling."

Humphries winked at the audience. "I should have been an art major."

Raskin raised an eyebrow and looked over to where Dean Melvin huddled near the door. The dean shrank against the doorframe, folding and unfolding his hands in a jittery routine. Standing next to him, Aurelia studied her nails, perhaps contemplating a new shade of acrylic. Both missed what Nicole and others saw behind them in the hallway.

Two strapping Iowa State Police officers prodded Bob Olufssen and detective Ronald Snife toward the building's entrance. The pair walked side by side, heads down, bright yellow nylon handcuffs binding them together in their misery.

"Was Bob working with DeTassell?" Nicole looked to Clark for an answer. He only shrugged.

Nicole watched in fascination as Bob resisted the police officers' attempts to move him past the dining room doors. He made a desperate attempt to reach for Aurelia and called out her name. The police officers jerked him away.

"Adios, muchachos." Clark watched the two prisoners disappear.

"Oh . . . my . . . God," Nicole dug her nails into Clark's arm. "Bob Olufssen is Aurelia's son."

"Not if you judge by her reaction." Clark pointed at Aurelia, who now stared straight ahead, without a glance at the disruption behind her. "Whoever said the Greeks were passé?"

At the front of the room, Humphries' voice boomed out. "The gentleman by my side possesses an enviable collection of O'Callaghan's early works and he saved many from falling into the hands of our enemy." Humphries paused and glanced at Raskin, as if waiting for a green light to complete the announcement.

Raskin inclined his head slightly.

Another grand smile lit up Humphries' face. "It boils down to this, folks. O'Callaghan paintings are now up for bid in several world art markets. Until recently, traveling incognito to London, Paris, and San Francisco among other destinations, always fearful for his safety, Dr. Raskin has negotiated sales of well over three million dollars. Now that he has secured the remainder of the paintings, our great friend has decided to donate millions to save this university."

A wild uproar among the faculty prevented Humphries' attempts to continue speaking. Professors yelled and hugged each other. In the back of the room, Haskell Simon and Sunny Wriston needed only the slightest excuse to glue their bodies together. Nicole averted her eyes for fear she'd be forever haunted by the couple's display.

Clark yelled at Nicole over the noise erupting throughout the room. "DeTassell had to get his hands on the rest of those paintings if he was going to get control of the University."

"What do you mean?"

"He knew they were worth enough to bail us out of debt." Clark moved close to Nicole so he didn't have to shout over the din. "I think Raskin must have stolen them back at the party. No wonder he fought so hard to keep hold of that map case. It was full of O'Callaghans."

Nicole knew he was right. She recalled how upset Raskin had been in the office at the beginning of the semester. He'd probably sold an

O'Callaghan painting in San Francisco, not expecting it would be reported in the newspapers. *I bet that's when he disappeared.*

Humphries cupped his hands over his mouth and shouted at the tumult before him. "One more minute of your attention, please."

For some reason, Aurelia employed her crowd control skills for the politician's benefit, bashing a food service samovar with a heavy metal candleholder. She smiled at nothing in particular, taking a healthy bite of her brownie as she banged away.

Humphries watched her with admiration.

Dean Melvin wrung his hands and tried his best to smile.

Jerry Atrect, sitting with his back to the samovar, snapped his fingers in tune with the racket immediately behind him.

"Dr. Raskin and I spoke with President Monarck just minutes before arriving here, and we hammered out the details of some new initiatives." Humphries drew a list from an interior pocket of his suit coat. "Starting tomorrow, Dr. Raskin will be named the founding director of the Higher State University Leisure Studies Program to be located in Nice, France. This is a new, fully endowed program."

Humphries' aide produced a red beret for Raskin, which he accepted graciously, waving it above his head several times to loud applause by the faculty. Politician and academic stood smiling together and taking turns wearing the beret for a crew of news photographers just arrived for the occasion.

"Aurelia Castle, this charming and accomplished woman to my left—" Humphries propped the beret back on Raskin's head and stepped quickly to Aurelia's side. "Ms. Castle will become my associate director of Campaign Affairs and Fund-Raising. She will have a special consultant's role on voter behavior in this district." Nicole could only imagine how the latter duties would intersect with university faculty and their voting behavior.

"Vote for my guy, or I'll stuff your freaking head in a samovar," said Horace.

"Finally, your distinguished dean, Arnold 'Buster' Melvin, will be reassigned." Humphries searched for another slip of paper in his suit jacket. At the hint of Dean Melvin's departure, faculty cheers thundered throughout the room.

Dean Melvin hunched his shoulders—a forlorn figure, a weary, helpless soul.

Humphries concluded a whispered conversation with Raskin and turned back to address the faculty. "Dean Melvin, despite some well-intentioned but misdirected attempts to save the university he loves so deeply, will now serve an important role at our new Institute of Plant Pharmacology. He will be there to witness the leading edge research first perfected at the former DeTassell Institute for Organic Farming."

Nicole watched in fascination as Dean Melvin rushed forward and hugged Scooter Humphries, clinging to him in unabashed joy, his feet swinging off the floor, resisting efforts by the politician's aide to detach him.

Raskin stood to the side of the whirling pair, having what Nicole could only imagine as a last laugh on the dean. If she judged Raskin's smile correctly, "Buster" Melvin would know the business end of a push broom better than anything else in his new position.

"The craziness. The craziness," Nicole whispered.

She had made up her mind.

I will not be here next semester.

CHAPTER 22

Under angled rays of winter sunshine, the Jetta raced up Interstate 35 toward the Minnesota state line. Approaching the Clear Lake exit, Nicole floored the accelerator, and the car responded with an unexpected burst of speed, flying by a semitrailer truck with "DeTassell Organic Produce" emblazoned in green letters on its side panel. Once past the truck, Nicole backed off the gas and the car's internal works produced a jumbo-sized cloud of exhaust smoke.

She patted the Jetta's dashboard, smiling at the trailing exhaust vapors obscuring any view out the rear window. "Très symbolique, eh, Jetta?"

The morning after the official end of the semester, Nicole packed her possessions into the car and set out for Minnesota. After some encouragement, Clark had agreed to keep Munchkin until Nicole found a place to stay in the Twin Cities.

Clark promised they would all be together soon, but didn't reveal what he had in mind. "Well, don't pick up any bad habits from Munchkin," Nicole teased as she and Clark said their good-byes.

"I promise not to stay out all night and never to be finicky about my dinner." Clark gave her that loopy smile she loved.

She already missed him.

Maintaining the speedometer at exactly seventy, Nicole tried to relax as the remaining miles to the Iowa-Minnesota border flew past. The trauma of final exam week had left Nicole and her colleagues little time to reflect on Professor Raskin's dramatic return. As faculty administered final exams, accepted term papers and projects, listened to students' questions, pleas, and excuses, and graded . . . graded . . . graded . . . the final faculty meeting, with its breathtaking finish, took a backseat to end-of-semester priorities.

Nicole didn't really care what happened now at Higher State, no matter what Raskin's reappearance meant for the university's future. She had to escape. The bizarre doings and daffy circumstances on the campus decided it. She couldn't imagine any changes that might cause her to stay.

She'd miss Horace, Sonja, Hildie, and Rubin. Poor Rubin. He'd had it once, the kind of idealism that drew Nicole toward teaching in the first place. But something had gone wrong. Nicole hoped she'd left Higher State to keep from losing those fragile threads of idealism that remained at semester's end. In her heart, she still wanted to be good college teacher. At the same time, the quality of the students in her classes bothered Nicole—made her ache to teach somewhere else.

Was that so wrong?

But if she was so committed to teaching, wouldn't she have found something to foster within each and every one of her students? She knew a few instructors who could, it seemed, feel the same way about every student . . . who worked as hard with the least talented as with the best.

Was that possible?

She wanted good students . . . graduate students someday. Damn it. She wanted a real place in the academy—a campus community of serious scholars her graduate work seemed to promise. She craved the intellectual excitement she'd experienced writing her dissertation. She dreamed of the academic big leagues—or at least the high minors.

Was that a stupid dream?

Her decision to leave Higher State would cost her. No job awaited in the Twin Cities, no guarantees of future prospects. Her student loan debts would still hang over her head. If worse came to worst, maybe she could find something else to do. She didn't have to stay in academic life, did she? There must be other careers . . .

Nicole recalled reading an article in the *Chronicle* about alternative careers for graduate students in the humanities, but never thought she'd have to pay attention to any of the suggestions. She also remembered a booklet from her undergraduate years about business careers for liberal arts majors. She'd thrown it away without a second thought. Maybe now was the time for a little research. There might be something worthwhile outside the ivory tower.

As she passed the "Welcome to Minnesota" sign, questions and doubts about the past semester nagged her. Always the good student, it was time to reflect.

What have we learned from this experience?

Despite all the discouraging moments of the past semester, she knew an answer to her question would be important. Her semester as a faculty member at Higher State had taught her things . . . about classroom teaching, about advising students, about faculty roles and responsibilities. Where did she need to improve? What lessons could she draw on for the future? She could make the last semester's experience count for something positive.

If only she had a textbook, a rubric, some debriefing questions to guide her reflection. She should be able to structure good questions. That's what philosophers do, isn't it?

She promised herself to write up a list.

One thing she knew for certain: her attitude about students needed adjusting. In her classes, she'd labored hard to hide her disappointments. As the semester progressed, she'd decided to concentrate her energies on the students who showed motivation and interest—no matter who, no matter how slight the manifestations. Despite initial mistakes and beginner's pratfalls in the classroom, Nicole had come to enjoy teaching her courses, and she really did care about most of her students.

The students seemed to think they had learned something from her.

To her surprise, she earned what seemed to be strong ratings on the instructor evaluations. According to the computer printout of survey results, her overall instructor rating was at 4.3 on a 5-point scale. Although Hildie had given her new strategies and ideas to try out in class, Nicole knew she hadn't changed her teaching that much. Her first semester had been far too busy for much experimentation and reflection. The good evaluations were a pleasant surprise.

She couldn't be sure what the students were thinking, but their written comments gave some clue: being "positive," "concerned about how students progressed in the class," "generally a fair grader," and Nicole's favorite, "giving me some good ethics." These comments went a long way to offset the few nasty notes scrawled by the minority in each class. Some of the negative comments did sting; many seemed inexplicable.

She wished the standardized evaluation form her classes filled out late in the semester told more about her teaching success or failure. But most of the response prompts didn't address the things Nicole could use to improve her teaching—especially her teaching of philosophy. She sympathized with untenured faculty at Higher State who would be judged, in part, by the results of the student evaluations. The university should come up with a new form.

"Back off, you jerk."

The tailgating yahoo in the pickup truck seemed only inches from her back bumper. Nicole took a quick look through the rearview mirror, but the mud and dirt encrusted on the Jetta's back window made it difficult to see anything more.

The pickup's driver blinked the headlights a couple of times and honked. Nicole worried about the possibility of a carjacking and kept driving at the speed limit. The Lakeville exit was only a few miles. She could get off there and drive directly to a gas station if this guy kept on her tail.

The pickup driver honked again and pulled out into the empty lane next to Nicole. She didn't dare look over.

Out of the corner of her eye, she detected some movement inside the pickup truck. A kitten had jumped up on the dashboard and struggled to keep its footing. The kitty looked a little like Munchkin.

It was Munchkin.

Clark and Nicole sat in a window booth inside the "Enfulfisk Diner and Ski Chalet," talking, drinking coffee, and holding hands across the table. They'd parked the Jetta and the pickup truck just outside the window by their booth. The Jetta's doors didn't lock, and Clark had stacked all his belongings into the bed of the pickup.

"I think we'll have more than enough to find a nice apartment," said Clark.

"But we'll need to buy a bed and stuff."

"We can handle that. No problem."

"I can't believe it. He gave you a check?"

Clark reached into his jacket pocket and slid a certified bank check across the table. "That's five zeroes you're counting after the numeral."

"It's like winning the lottery."

"We are the first and last R. Reynolds Raskin Faculty Scholars." Clark waggled his eyebrows. "Who'd have thunk it? The old boy was so happy I'd saved the sketch O'Callaghan did of him, he almost hugged me."

Nicole and Clark made plans to stop at her dad's house for a late dinner and headed outside. The temperature had already dropped well below Minnesota requirements for a mid-December early evening. Nicole dreaded sitting on the Jetta's leather seat, which by now had stored a goodly amount of the freezing air—enough to give even the hardiest Minnesotan a wicked jolt.

"I'll follow you over to your dad's house." Clark stood with his back to the pickup's front window.

Nicole stepped forward and wrapped her arms around his neck. She held him tight. A few inches away, Munchkin scratched at the frosty inside of the window, meowing . . . her eyes narrowed, fixed on Clark's neck.

THE MISSING PROFESSOR

THE MISSING PROFESSOR

Informal Case Studies/Discussion Stories
for Faculty Development, New Faculty
Orientation, and Campus Conversations

Thomas B. Jones

STERLING, VIRGINIA

Sty/us

COPYRIGHT © 2006 STYLUS PUBLISHING, LLC

Published by Stylus Publishing, LLC
22883 Quicksilver Drive
Sterling, Virginia 20166-2102

Library of Congress Cataloging-in-Publication Data
Jones, Thomas B., 1942–
    The missing professor : an academic mystery :
informal case studies, discussion stories for faculty
development, new faculty orientation, and campus
conversations / Thomas B. Jones.—1st ed.
        p.   cm.
    ISBN 1-57922-137-8 (hardcover : alk. paper)
    ISBN 1-57922-138-6 (pbk. : alk. paper)
    1. College personnel management.   2. Teacher-
administrator relationships.   I. Title.
LB2331.66.J66   2005
378.1′2—dc22   2005020833

ISBN: 1-57922-137-8 (cloth)
ISBN: 1-57922-138-6 (paper)

Printed in Canada

All first editions printed on acid-free paper
that meets the American National Standards Institute
Z39-48 Standard.

First Edition, 2006

10   9   8   7   6   5   4   3   2   1

Contents

Introduction

The Missing Professor offers a simple, fun way for busy faculty (advisors and administrators as well) to meet and talk about things that matter. Throughout this book, I have attempted to include important issues and dilemmas faced by college and university faculty members, regardless of age, rank, or academic discipline.

I hope the informal case studies and stories contained in *The Missing Professor* will (1) break down a number of academic barriers (among disciplines, for example), (2) draw on a range of professional and personal experiences, (3) promote spirited discussions, and (4) fit with several development goals—such as new-faculty orientation, mentoring, teaching improvement, and student advising.

My experience with informal case study/discussion stories has convinced me faculty will need few if any prompts to launch into vigorous discussions. No worry about "pulling teeth" to get things started. We are, after all, highly trained professionals, aren't we?

As faculty members read through this book—filtering each chapter through their experiences and expertise—they will identify new questions and issues for discussion. So, this section of *The Missing Professor* is not designed as a full-blown user's guide or an elaborate road map for discussions.

Anyone interested in doing some background reading for the cases and stories will find a sizable number of books, articles, Web sites, and other resources. For a "quick and dirty" solution, I would recommend searching through publications and journals such as *The Chronicle of Higher Education, Change Magazine, The National Forum for Teaching and Learning, The Teaching Professor, The Journal of Excellence in College Teaching*, and *College Teaching*. Browsing through books and journals from publishers with an interest in higher education and teaching, like Anker Press, Jossey-Bass, or Stylus Publishing, will lead to the most recent research and issues. The growing number of first-rate college and university Web sites devoted to teaching and faculty development offer a treasure trove of useful materials and links to other resources. Time spent surfing through these Web sites will yield several favorites. A good place to start searching is the lists supplied by Dalhousie University's Office of Instructional Development and Technology and the University of Kansas' Center for Teaching Excellence.

Almost every chapter of *The Missing Professor* places Nicole Adams and her colleagues at Higher State University in situations where they face a range of dilemmas and challenges. What follows is a chapter-by-chapter rundown of potential cases and discussion issues. I have provided a series of questions to help initiate and focus discussions.

Thomas B. Jones
Kansas City, Missouri
July 2005

CASE STUDIES AND DISCUSSION ISSUES

Note: Chapters 11, 14, 16, 18, and 21 are not designed for discussions.

Chapters 1–2—Decision to accept a first academic position; graduate school preparation for the job market; first-year choices about research, teaching, and service; finding employment information; preparing for classes; sexual harassment.

Chapter 3—Teaching the first class; student–teacher communication and classroom problems; finding useful information about students.

Chapter 4—Serving on faculty committees; peer evaluation of teaching; effective teaching; classroom assessment; interacting with students.

Chapter 5—Student incivility (problems, causes, instructor responses).

Chapter 6—Faculty governance (issues and problems); academic decision making; accrediting associations; assessment concerns.

Chapter 7—Administration/faculty power and decision-making authority; faculty "responsibility."

Chapter 8—Admission standards and open admissions; students at varying levels of preparation and ability; reading assignments; adapting and changing teaching approaches.

Chapter 9—Credits for prior experiential learning; measuring and evaluating learning; adult learners.

Chapter 10—Student issues; testing and grading; encouraging students; complaints and excuses.

Chapter 12—"Academic equal rights" and student indoctrination; faculty and student "commitments and obligations."

Chapter 13—Faculty and administrators' roles; the scholarship of teaching and learning; classroom research.

Chapter 15—Tenure and public perceptions; tenure and nontenured/adjunct professors; tenure and academic freedom; alternatives to tenure?

Chapter 17—Why go to college? The value of a college degree; the collegiate experience.

1

Chapters 19–20—Reforming general education; models for general education; students and general education requirements; teaching and general education.

Chapter 22—Careers outside academe; new faculty (assessing and reflecting on experiences); student ratings of instruction.

DISCUSSION QUESTIONS

Chapter 1

1. Nicole Adams is having second thoughts about her new position at Higher State. What would you advise her to do? How do personal and academic values shape your advice?
2. Is it your experience that graduate professors and advisors have a good sense of "the market" and career possibilities for their students? Do graduate students have the preparation and training to deal successfully with the demands of job seeking?
3. What advice would you offer to a graduate student in your field setting out in the academic job market?
4. What sorts of issues and problems facing new faculty would you list if Nicole were starting her employment at your institution? What would be on your list of things to discuss and to do if you were Nicole's faculty mentor?
5. As a new faculty member at your campus, would Nicole have any specific protections and resources available to help her adjust and make decisions? What would you see as necessary additions to existing protections and resources?
6. Will a new faculty member at your campus be forced to sacrifice research and writing because of a heavy teaching load, committee responsibilities, and the lack of a major research library? Will a new faculty member be at a disadvantage when applying for fellowships and grants? What would you advise a new faculty member to do about research and writing ambitions and balancing teaching, research, and service in the first few years?

Chapter 2

1. Put yourself in Nicole's shoes for this first day of classes. What would you do in response to encounters with the likes of Professor Raskin and Ted, the would-be philosophy major?
2. If you were Nicole's office partner, what would you tell her about getting started as an instructor and as a department member? What sorts of responsibilities does a departmental colleague have with regard to a new faculty member?
3. How might a new faculty member go about negotiating a balance among the demands of teaching, research, and service before signing a contract?
4. What would you advise a new faculty member to know about your university's policies on tenure, promotion, and service? Where would a new faculty member find good sources of information and advice about such things on your campus?
5. What would you advise a new faculty member to do in preparation for teaching classes on your campus? Which of these preparations do you think will prove most important and effective?
6. What are the possibilities in your situation for pursuing research that would be in close harmony with what you are teaching? What are the pros and cons of doing so?

Chapter 3

1. How would you evaluate Nicole's approach to her first class session? What should she know about the importance of the first class and how to go about teaching it?
2. What would you recommend as the most important preparations and actions teachers should consider for the first meeting of a class? What sort of a checklist would you recommend to Nicole for constructing an effective syllabus?
3. What approach would you recommend as most effective for the first few minutes of class as the semester begins?
4. Electronic classrooms are becoming a common element of college teaching. On the basis of your experience and study, what are the pros and cons of such technology for the classroom?
5. How might Nicole better deal with some of the situations she faces in this first class? What is the connection, if any, between Nicole's teaching approach and students' behavior?
6. How did the end-of-class group exercise go wrong? How would you set up and handle this group exercise?
7. What might Nicole do at the next class meeting as damage control?
8. What should she attempt to learn about her students? What sources of information about students can you use at your campus? How can you construct a better portrait of students in your classes? How will the information you have available help improve teaching and learning in your classes?

Chapter 4

1. What sort of training is necessary for someone engaging in peer reviews of teaching?
2. Based on what you know about Bob Olufssen's class, how might you evaluate his teaching? Is his teaching approach likely to be effective? Why might students like his approach? What can Nicole learn from Bob's teaching?
3. What will Bob gain from the classroom assessment questions he asks? Is his question "How could you apply today's learning to a situation you might meet outside this classroom?" a good one?
4. What's your opinion of Bob's interactions with his students?
5. Take a look at the Classroom Evaluation Form opposite. Would you feel comfortable with this form and its questions if applied to your teaching? What changes would you suggest?
6. Should Bob be allowed to add any information and observations to the peer evaluation form? Will the process yield a fair and reliable evaluation of Bob's teaching? Should there be additional steps in the process?
7. How are peer evaluations of teaching conducted on your campus? Are there other approaches to peer evaluation of teaching that might be more effective and appropriate?

Higher State University

"PUSH THE PEDAGOGY" CLASSROOM EVALUATION FORM

Please write your responses to questions 1–5 on the sheets provided with this packet:

1. **Does this instructor have a strong command of the subject he/she is teaching?** (Demonstrates a solid understanding/command of the subject matter for the course, has up-to-date knowledge; makes clear distinctions between fact and opinion; presents material worth knowing; promotes the acquisition of factual knowledge and fundamental principles, generalizations, or theories)
2. **Has this instructor prepared and organized this course appropriately?** (Syllabus and objectives allow students a clear overview of the course and materials to be covered; organizes presentations in an effective way and at an appropriate pace; organizes class session so that students can connect learning to previously studied materials and future directions)
3. **Does the instructor work well with students?** (Encourages learning and active participation in the class; holds the interest of students and earns their respect; displays a concern for student learning and development; is sensitive to student learning problems and points of view)
4. **How well does the instructor manage his/her classroom?** (Creates a nonthreatening learning atmosphere; is sensitive to students' differences; promptly and effectively deals with student misbehavior; meets class at scheduled time and is prepared to begin class; ends class in a timely manner)
5. **How effective are the instructional techniques used by this instructor?** (Uses a variety of teaching techniques, materials, and forms of presentation; communicates clearly and effectively; promotes class discussion as appropriate and asks questions to stimulate discussions; demonstrates enthusiasm for subject; makes class challenging, thought provoking, and interesting; encourages critical thinking)

Comments on instructor's strengths and weaknesses?
Summary comments and recommendations for improvement?

Chapter 5

Note: "A Survey on Academic Incivility at Indiana University," which includes sample questions, would be a good preface to discussing the issue raised in this chapter. Go to www.Indiana.edu/~csr/Civility%20PreReport.pdf.

1. Like Nicole, faculty in various situations may find it necessary to set some boundaries (for other faculty colleagues, administrators, and students) to protect their private lives. What are some clear and reasonable boundaries? How would you go about setting these boundaries with faculty colleagues and others at your campus who fail to recognize your need for privacy?
2. How would you define student incivility?
3. Are incidents of student incivility in the college classroom on the rise? If so, how do you explain the increase?
4. Which of the incidents in Professor Porter's class do you consider to be examples of student incivility?
5. Does Professor Porter contribute in any way to the student problems he faces? Are some teachers more likely to experience student incivility?
6. What course of action would you recommend to Professor Porter in response to student incivility? What can he do in terms of planning his class sessions and teaching strategies to deal with the problems he faces?
7. Are there conditions and situations in a classroom where student incivility is more likely to occur? Which causes can be traced to faculty approaches to teaching and their interactions with students?
8. How should Professor Porter respond to the two students who disrupt class at the end of the period? Was it a "teaching moment"?
9. How would you structure a student code of conduct to help deal with student incivility at Higher State University? What do you think would be critical to the success of such a student code of conduct?

Chapter 6

1. Typically, what are the problems and issues surrounding faculty governance at your institution? How are decisions made at your college and university? What is the role and responsibility for individual faculty members in matters of decision making at these levels (department, division, campuswide)?
2. What factors do you think led originally to the emphasis on assessment in higher education? What do you know about the role, powers, and philosophy of your regional accrediting association?
3. What does the faculty meeting in this chapter reveal about the awareness and understanding of assessment at Higher State? Who has the responsibility on your campus for educating faculty and others about assessment?
4. What causes most faculty to be suspicious of assessment and resist efforts to establish assessment programs?
5. In the story, does the opponent of assessment identify legitimate issues and criticisms? Would any of these issues and criticisms apply at your institution? Is assessment a threat to academic freedom?
6. What about grading and assessment? Should course grades be used as assessment evidence? What are the pros and cons of an assessment system focused on the classroom and department level?

Chapter 7

1. What would be the most striking similarities and differences between the faculty meeting portrayed in this chapter and a faculty meeting at your institution? What would you identify as reasons for the similarities and differences?

2. What might administrators on your campus cite as frustrations and stumbling blocks they face in terms of faculty governance? What might faculty on your campus identify as frustrations and stumbling blocks in working with administration? What attitudes and actions on both sides might cause these problems? What are the possible solutions?

3. Is it possible or necessary to identify an appropriate division of power and decision making between faculty and administration in an "urgent" situation?

4. How would you define "leadership," "management," and "administration" on your campus? Can you offer specific examples that help define specific skills in each of the above? How do these skills translate into your everyday work?

5. Is Dean Melvin's request for "reasonable dispatch" and for faculty "to translate their decisions from words to actions and responsibility" appropriate? What might be some of the factors that impede faculty from doing the tasks requested?

6. For better or worse, are there types of faculty who serve on multiple committees and hold elected faculty positions for long terms? What are the potential consequences of this practice? What roles are appropriate for new faculty to take in governance and decision making?

7. How important are department chairs when it comes to decision making at your institution? Do they tend to be the most powerful bloc within the faculty and most respected by administrators? Why? Pros and cons?

Chapter 8

1. If you were in a classroom situation, teaching students with a wide disparity of skills, how would you proceed? Do you find significant differences among students in your classes in terms of preparation and potential? How do you deal with these differences as an instructor? What are your strategies and approaches?
2. Are the problems described in the story accurate? In day-to-day classroom situations, what is the effect of these problems? For students? For teachers?
3. A general complaint among many college teachers is that students do not read as much (or as competently) as those of past generations. Is this your impression? What might be an explanation for the decline? How might this make a difference in the way you teach? How should teachers deal with students who do not keep up with the reading assignments?
4. What is your response to student excuses for missing assignments? What are some possible strategies to deal with such problems?
5. How should teachers go about making changes and experimenting with regard to classroom instruction? What might be the causes of Rubin's failures with group strategies?

Chapter 9

Note: As an introduction to this discussion issue, go to www.metrostate.edu/fc/cls.html for one approach to prior learning assessment and theory seminars.

1. Does it make a difference where and how learning occurs in terms of granting college credits if the outcomes are verifiable at a college level?
2. What are your thoughts about granting college credit for learning acquired outside the classroom? Is it possible for students at your campus to receive credit for prior experiential learning?
3. Greater numbers of experienced adult learners now involved in higher education have measurable, college-level learning experiences. Will receiving credit for this learning enhance the quality of their degree programs?
4. Why do you think that most colleges and universities have been reluctant to grant credit for prior experiential learning or to expand such programs?
5. What are the practical and political issues on your campus for adopting (or expanding) a system for crediting prior learning?
6. If your institution grants credit for prior learning experiences, which academic departments, programs, and courses feel the most impact? Who makes decisions about granting such credits and what criteria are used in decision making?
7. What should faculty consider about how students learn when it comes to adults and traditional age groups of college students? What should faculty know about successfully teaching adult learners?
8. What are the pros and cons of teaching classes with a mix of traditional-age students and adult students? What are some successful teaching approaches for such classes?

Chapter 10

1. How do you handle students who, though motivated and attempting to work up to their abilities, still struggle to succeed? Where would you send students to find help on your campus other than what you can provide?
2. How would you respond to Ashley in the story? Was allowing students to use their notes in the middle of the exam appropriate?
3. How can Nicole address some of the problems she is experiencing with student motivation and study habits? How would you model for students what it takes to be a successful learner in your discipline or subject area?
4. What policies outlined on a syllabus could help prevent the student excuses Nicole is hearing? How would you word a syllabus to deal with (a) makeups for missed exams, (b) late assignments, and (c) absences?
5. How do you prepare students to do well on your exams?
6. What would you suggest to Nicole about grading response essays for best results? What is a rubric? What are the advantages of constructing rubrics for grading and assessing learning?
7. What are the possibilities in your discipline or subject to cut down the time spent grading without sacrificing evaluations necessary for learning?

Chapter 12

Note: The Academic Bill of Rights can be found by searching www.students foracademicfreedom.org or www.frontpagemag.com.

1. Has your campus experienced conflicts about "academic fairness" or heard requests to adjust hiring of faculty to balance political bias?
2. Are the demands for an Academic Equal Rights Act or the enhancement of "intellectual diversity" necessary for higher education? On your campus? Within your department or academic unit?
3. Is Professor Dufer correct in his assertion that liberals and the left dominate higher education? Are students being indoctrinated? What might you advise students about classroom situations they perceive to be "indoctrination"?
4. Is it realistic to think that colleges and universities can construct a balance of political viewpoints in classrooms and in departments?
5. Is a listing of faculty "commitments and expectations" a reasonable undertaking? What might such a listing accomplish? Does it have any potential advantages for better defining faculty roles and responsibilities? What are the problems associated with such a listing?
6. If you were to draw up a list of commitments to and expectations of students, what would it look like?

Chapter 13

Note: For an introduction to the scholarship of teaching and learning (SOTL), go to www.carnegiefoundation.org/CASTL. This site also has Dr. Pat Hutchins' annotated bibliography on SOTL.

1. What approaches and strategies would you recommend for faculty at your institution to best manage the many demands on their time?

2. Nicole has witnessed quite a sampling of destructive behaviors by faculty and administrators as they pursue professional duties outside the classroom and work with students. What key issues and questions would you add to those recognized by Nicole in her reflections? How have faculty and administrators on your campus attempted to deal with some of these troublesome issues and questions?

3. Given Nicole's experiences with quarreling faculty and administrators, cynicism, and so on, what are the implications you can identify for mentoring new faculty, retention of faculty, self-renewal, and holding on to ideals and priorities in a similar situation?

4. In the context of daily duties and challenges faced by faculty and administrators as professionals, how can they avoid losing control of their "better selves"?

5. Go to http://titans.iusb.edu/josotl/search_archives.htm and read some of the papers archived at that site. How do these project reports compare with your ideas about the scholarship of teaching and learning as a branch of scholarship within higher education?

6. How do you (would you) go about measuring the "character and depth" of students' learning? Is this measurement necessary to good teaching? Should the assessment of student learning be a component of a teaching portfolio or teaching evaluation?

7. As defined, does this scholarship of teaching and learning seem to be on a par with the scholarship of discovery? Of application? Of integration? What distinguishes the scholarship of teaching and learning from research in educational psychology?

8. Is research on teaching and learning possible without significant

training in statistics, educational psychology, and similar areas, or collaboration with someone in those fields?

9. What are some of the issues and problems associated with conducting classroom research? What are the rules your discipline and/ or campus have established for such research?

10. If you were Lenore Sedgwick, hoping to involve more faculty in a consideration of the scholarship of teaching and learning, how would you structure a workshop on the subject: (a) to respond to the challenge posed by Professor Bierman, and (b) to allow him and his colleagues opportunities to find something they will value by attending the workshop?

Chapter 15

Note: This chapter follows on Dr. C. Peter Magrath's "Point of View" essay on tenure published in *The Chronicle of Higher Education* (February 28, 1997), A60, in addition to the online debate that followed.

1. What are some situations in which tenure might protect a professor at your campus from outside political pressures?
2. Is it the case that most people outside of academic life do not understand or support the idea of tenure? If so, what are some of the public's perceptions about tenure? What are some of the most common objections?
3. Should tenured professors enjoy a protected status now denied to nontenured and part-time faculty, who often teach the majority of classes offered at many colleges and universities?
4. How would you assess Scooter Humphries' point that protections provided by the First Amendment are sufficient for faculty in higher education?
5. As some argue, could enhanced contractual language provide the protections necessary for faculty as opposed to a tenure system? Compare the advantages and disadvantages of tenure with the protections provided by unionization, collective bargaining agreements, or extending civil service status to faculty members.
6. How would you defend tenure to a parent or community critic of the system?

Chapter 17

1. The future earning power of a college degree is a strong selling point for higher education. What factors might segment and restrict this promise of a college degree for many students?
2. If the undergraduate college degree promises fewer rewards these days for certain majors and fields, what sorts of adjustments are necessary, if any, in teaching and advising students?
3. Is Nicole correct in thinking that students at most any college and university can acquire a good education through careful selection of courses and professors? If so, how would you advise a student to go about this process of selection at your campus?
4. What are (or should be) the roles and responsibilities of faculty members for issues of student life outside the classroom? Do you agree with Nicole's answer to Jamal, "it's something students have to work out for themselves"?
5. How would you revise and extend the College Board's *Why Get a College Degree* explanation?
6. How would you respond to the challenges and questions Jamal raises in his visit with Nicole? What would you write in a letter to Jamal if you were Nicole? Why should Jamal go to college now instead of later?
7. Jamal asks, "What made you all gung ho about college? What is this special thing about being a college student?" How would you answer his questions on the basis of your own undergraduate experiences?

Chapter 19

Note: The basis for this case comes from an article by Gordon Arnold and Janet T. Civian, "The Ecology of General Education Reform," in *Change Magazine* (July–August 1997), 18–24, and Barry Latzer's "Point of View" essay on general education in *The Chronicle of Higher Education* (October 8, 2004), B20.

1. What lies behind changes and reforms in general education throughout higher education over the past fifteen years?
2. Why would you urge faculty on your campus to have ongoing discussions about general education? How would you structure such conversations for the best results?
3. What problems might result from borrowing and adapting another institution's approach to general education as a model for your curriculum?
4. Why is general education reform often so difficult? What are the potential costs of reforming general education in terms of time and money? Which groups and factions on a campus are most likely to support general education reform? Which would be most likely to oppose such reform?
5. At your campus are most general education courses taught by junior faculty and adjuncts? What are the implications of such a practice if true?
6. What do most students on your campus think about general education (purposes and goals, requirements, courses, and instruction)? Do most students see general education as a "ticket-punching exercise"?
7. How does your institution prepare students to have a stronger understanding of general education before they progress very far down the road of requirements? Does your orientation for new students include a session on general education?
8. Do you agree that the educated person question is at the heart of a general education program? Would a course like Higher State's "Educated Person" be applicable to your curriculum?
9. How are the strengths of your institution incorporated in your

general education plan? How is general education linked to liberal education at your campus?

10. How do you measure the effectiveness of your general education requirements, courses, and instruction? What have you learned?

Chapter 20

1. Are most general education programs compatible and relevant to the needs of students in the twenty-first century? What do you think of Dean Melvin's "four frameworks": basic literacy, technological literacy, visual literacy, and marketplace literacy? How would you revise or extend these broad frameworks?
2. What role should the traditional liberal arts disciplines play in general education? Are the liberal arts disciplines the core or centerpiece of any general education experience? What are the understandings, skills, and methods contributed by the liberal arts disciplines to students involved in general education coursework?
3. Are some of those disciplines more fundamental than others to the success of students' general education experience? Are certain courses indispensable to the success of general education?
4. Is it possible for courses associated with professional education (for example, marketing or statistics) to contribute to a liberal education? What is the role that faculty and departments in technical and professional fields should play as contributors to a liberal education?
5. What do you think is most important to the success of a general education program—who teaches in it and specific courses required, or how the general education program is constructed as an overall curriculum?

Chapter 22

1. Is Nicole's dream career realistic for the vast majority of graduate students? If you were advising a graduate student starting an academic job search, what would be your advice (for example, where to apply, preparing applications, interviewing, and so on)?

2. A good liberal education (or liberal learning outcomes) should provide someone like Nicole with the ability to discover and qualify for broader career opportunities in both academic and nonacademic settings. What potential career possibilities are there outside of teaching or academic life for someone like Nicole? What skills and understandings might she have as a result of her undergraduate and graduate study that would be useful in a nonacademic career and attractive to an employer? Where would you suggest she find more information and advice about careers outside academe?

3. What would you include on a list of questions for new faculty interested in reflecting on their first year as a professor? What categories would you suggest for such a reflection? Based on your experience, how would you answer some of the questions Nicole has posed?

4. Do you share some of the same disappointments Nicole has about the quality of her students? How might she "adjust" her attitudes and be more realistic about teaching the majority of her students?

5. Take a look at the IDEA papers numbers 20–33, and the information on student ratings of instructors at the IDEA Center, at www.idea.ksu.edu/index.html. Can course evaluations and instructor ratings confirm that someone is a good teacher? How do you view the usefulness and validity of such ratings? What are some alternatives for teachers who want more feedback on their teaching and courses?

6. How does your campus rating form compare with Higher State's (see form opposite)? What do you see as the strengths and weaknesses of the Higher State rating form? What questions would you add? What sorts of questions and rating categories do you find most helpful for improving your teaching?

7. Beyond student ratings, what other measures would you recommend for faculty personnel decisions (for salary, tenure, and promotion) at your institution? What relative weight should be assigned to student ratings in a system of multiple measures?

Higher State University
Student Evaluation of Instruction

The instructor has a broad knowledge and command of the subject matter
Strongly Agree   **Agree**   **Neutral**   **Disagree**   **Strongly Disagree**

The instructor has set clear objectives and goals for the course
Strongly Agree   **Agree**   **Neutral**   **Disagree**   **Strongly Disagree**

The instructor was well organized and prepared for class
Strongly Agree   **Agree**   **Neutral**   **Disagree**   **Strongly Disagree**

The instructor stimulated students' interest in learning the subject matter
Strongly Agree   **Agree**   **Neutral**   **Disagree**   **Strongly Disagree**

The instructor's oral and/or visual presentations were clear
Strongly Agree   **Agree**   **Neutral**   **Disagree**   **Strongly Disagree**

Class sessions began on time
Strongly Agree   **Agree**   **Neutral**   **Disagree**   **Strongly Disagree**

Class sessions ended on time
Strongly Agree   **Agree**   **Neutral**   **Disagree**   **Strongly Disagree**

The assignments, tests, and exams were fair
Strongly Agree   **Agree**   **Neutral**   **Disagree**   **Strongly Disagree**

Tests and assignments were returned promptly
Strongly Agree   **Agree**   **Neutral**   **Disagree**   **Strongly Disagree**

The instructor was available for assistance outside of the class
Strongly Agree   **Agree**   **Neutral**   **Disagree**   **Strongly Disagree**

The instructor treats students fairly, and with dignity and respect
Strongly Agree   **Agree**   **Neutral**   **Disagree**   **Strongly Disagree**

The textbooks and other materials were useful in understanding the course
Strongly Agree   **Agree**   **Neutral**   **Disagree**   **Strongly Disagree**

I rate the teaching effectiveness of this instructor as
Excellent   **Very Good**   **Good**   **Below Average**   **Poor**

On the other side of this sheet, please provide written comments on the things you liked best or liked least about this course. Additional comments are welcome.